VOICES *of* EASTLEIGH

GLEN JAYSON

To Mum

Happy Mothers Day 2012
from
Anne-Marie
and Andy.

Happy Reading — Glen Jayson
x

The History Press

The author, Glen Jayson.

To Tony

First published 2012

The History Press
The Mill, Brimscombe Port
Stroud, Gloucestershire, GL5 2QG
www.thehistorypress.co.uk

British Library Cataloguing in Publication Data.
A catalogue record for this book is available from the British Library.

ISBN 978 0 7524 6301 8

Typesetting and origination by The History Press
Printed in Great Britain
Manufacturing managed by Jellyfish Print Solutions Ltd

CONTENTS

INTRODUCTION

In this book you will meet people whose ages range from 103 down to seven. Their reminiscences may start from pre-Second World War days and some recall family background in the early twentieth century. Others talk about the 1960s onwards and life today. History is in the making every day and by the time this reaches the bookshop, comments on the present will be history. Hopes for the future may have materialised.

No interviewee can claim complete accuracy (we all have 'senior moments'). They are an individual's point of view and memory and while I have written up their stories as accurately as possible, apologies are given for any discrepancies.

These are stories of people's lives in the Borough of Eastleigh; to me the warmth of their personalities shines through, something they attribute to being brought up in what was once a close railway community. I hope you enjoy reading about them as much as I had the pleasure of meeting them.

ALL ABOUT EASTLEIGH

Eastleigh is a town 6 miles from Southampton city centre and 4 from Winchester. The Borough of Eastleigh was formed in 1973 and includes the following parishes:

Chandler's Ford and Hiltingbury
Eastleigh
Hedge End, West End and Botley
Bishopstoke, Fair Oak and Horton Heath
Bursledon, Hamble-le-Rice and Hound (Netley)

Before 1868, there was no town called Eastleigh. Pre-1840 it was a rural area of little more than three farms: Barton Peveril, Little Eastley and Great Eastley. There was a hamlet called North Stoneham to the south and a village called Bishopstoke in the east. 'Eastleigh' was officially named in 1868 by Charlotte Yonge, a novelist from nearby Otterbourne, because the Domesday Book describes the area by that name.

Eastleigh today is no dead railway town. There are many retail, industrial and business parks. At the leafy Hampshire Corporate Park in Chandler's Ford you'll find Norwich Union, Aviva and the B&Q Head Office. The Tollgate comprises many administration centres including Ageas. The Swan Centre in Wells Place contains a library, bowling alley and a multiplex cinema as well as a wide range of shops and coffee houses.

Population

Year	Population	Year	Population
1841	80	1931	16,069
1861	253	1951	30,559
1881	1,017	1971	77,966
1901	7,779	1981	92,140
1921	15,613	2001	116,169

Seven Famous People Linked to Eastleigh

Tommy Green	1894–1975	Olympic Gold Medallist, 50km walk, 1932
Sir Arthur Young	1907–79	Commissioner, City of London Police
Vince Hawkins	1923–8	Champion boxer
Benny Hill	1924–97	Comedian/actor
Heinz Burt	1942–2000	Pop star, musician
Colin Firth	1960–	Actor
Scott Mills	1974–	Radio DJ

Important Dates (to 1974)

1839   Opening of Nine Elms railway station, Battersea, London, as terminus of London & Southampton Railway (name changed to L&SWR (London & South Western Railway). First train ran from Northam (Southampton) to Winchester.

1840   London to Southampton railway line opened, with Bishopstoke station a changing point for Portsmouth.

1847   Line added to Romsey and Salisbury. Station becomes an important junction, called Bishopstoke Junction (until 1852), Bishopstoke & Eastleigh (until 1889) then Eastleigh in 1923.

1848   Nine Elms station was inconvenient for central London so the L&SWR constructed a metropolitan extension to Waterloo Bridge station.

1870   Eastleigh's first school was built, renamed in 1936 as Crescent School.

1886   Waterloo Bridge station was officially shortened to 'Waterloo'.

1886   The carriage and wagon works moved from Nine Elms to Eastleigh.

1892   L&SWR built the Railway Institute for its employees' recreation.

1893   Local Parish Board was replaced by Eastleigh Urban District Council.

1896   The council obtained Recreation Field and laid it out as a park.

1899   The council merged with neighbouring Bishopstoke.

1903   Locomotive cleaning and running sheds moved from Northam.

1909   The locomotive works moved from Nine Elms.

1910   Edwin Moon flew his monoplane called *Moonbeam* from a field in North Stoneham Farm.

1911   The first cinema opened.

1917   North Stoneham Farm was made into a military airfield

1921   Pirelli General Cable Works was established.

1920s First council houses were built in Winchester Road and Derby Road.

1928   The town hall was built.

1930s Causton & Sons Ltd, printers & stationery manufacturers, opened a large factory.

1936   The Spitfire's maiden flight took place from the airport. Also, the first Eastleigh Borough was incorporated.

1937   Prices Bakery opened.

1945   The construction began of the large council estate built on the northern side of Fleming Park.

1962   Dr Beeching announced plans to close the wagon and carriage works. Despite protests, the plans went ahead. Only the locomotive works remained.

1970s Private housing estates were built in many areas, such as Boyatt Wood, Fair Oak and Hedge End.

1972   The Local Government Act declared Eastleigh Borough was to merge with seven parishes from Winchester Rural District.

1973   The new Borough of Eastleigh came into effect.

Edwin Moon taking off in his monoplane Moonbeam *at North Stoneham Farm. (Solent Sky)*

An aerial view of the Pirelli factory, Leigh Road, 1930s. (Eastleigh Borough Council)

THE AUTHOR'S VIEW OF EASTLEIGH

When I moved to Highfield, Southampton, in 1970, Eastleigh often seemed more convenient than central Southampton. Parking was easier and free and our favourite Saturday afternoon pastime was to visit Jack Hobbs' record shop in the High Street. I can still visualise those tatty cardboard boxes containing second-hand albums. That lovely feel of glossy 12in LP covers as you flicked through hoping to find the album you couldn't afford brand new.

When the children came along, it was the cosy Regal where we had the excuse to watch Disney films again. When Fleming Park Sports Centre opened we much preferred to go there. The baby pool was separated from the main pool by a reinforced glass partition, much quieter for toddlers, and also the water was warm.

Today, like all towns now, parking is no longer easy or free and modern blocks of flats are springing up everywhere – but I still like Eastleigh. I like the lived-in feel to the place and find the people friendly, although some life-long residents say it has lost the friendliness. The Point, which was once the town hall, is a particularly good and busy arts centre and I like the colonnades in the main streets, especially when it's pouring with rain. At Christmas time, the festive street lights are a cheerful sight.

ARTHUR BANKS

Arthur, aged 103, is a volunteer at Rodbard House Day Centre
where he likes to help the elderly.

My son worked in Southampton and thought it best that my wife Kitty and I moved near to them. We were attracted to Netley, being on the shore of Southampton Water, so on Christmas Eve 1982 we left London and arrived at Alan Chun House. Our flat is on the second floor and the lift wasn't working. The removal men weren't too pleased and charged us extra.

We settled in well. There were lots of activities to take part in. There is less now, I expect because of the recession and some residents getting older and more frail. There's four of us left who continue with a card night.

North Stoneham village school in 1910. Arthur Banks was three years old then. (Len Harvell)

Arthur Banks, aged 103, pictured at Rodbard House Day Centre, Lowford, where he is a volunteer, helping the elderly.

Kitty used the day centre here when she became ill so I volunteered to help out and carried on after she passed away. I've been going once a week for eighteen years, although the Day Centre moved to different premises when the oven stopped working. I work mainly in the kitchen. First thing, I get the kettle on and the trolley sorted with cups, saucers and plates of biscuits. I don't carry cups of tea to people, I let someone else do that. Then it's heating the plates ready for dinner, setting the tables, serving the dinner, more cups of tea and washing up. At two o'clock I have a sit down. There is usually entertainment or games arranged for the afternoon before going home at 3.30. That might not sound exhausting or much fun to a young man but believe me – age slows you down.

Kitty and I loved dancing and went to a lot of dance clubs. I still like a dance but there aren't many suitable places around now. Sadly the church round the corner is about to close their dancing afternoon – not much demand for ballroom dancing, they say. Last Saturday I went to Fareham on the bus. To my delight, there was a belly dancing display in the precinct with about twelve women shimmying around. Yes, I really enjoyed that.

The oldest people I know are ninetyish. Being born in 1907 is a strange feeling, a bit 'on the shelf'. I get some help cleaning the flat but cook for myself. Sometimes its ready meals from the freezer, but I do appreciate having my own choice of what to eat.

GORDON DAUBNEY COX

as described by Len Sheldon

Gordon (1912–2008), who wrote books about Eastleigh, would visit the Town Clerk's Office in the 1960s when he was organiser of the twinning association with Villeneuve. His voice was quite loud when he spoke on the phone to his French counterpart, Madame Noblet. This continued after the move to the Civic Offices. He'd hold a high-decibel chat with the French, getting frustrated because they seemed laid back about what was happening and when. Gord usually sorted it even if his visits were sometimes a teensy bit disruptive in the open plan environment. But the one-sided French conversation was always worth listening to!

Gordon bubbled with enthusiasm about everything he was involved in. His knowledge of local people and places and his willingness to help find historical information was invaluable. This never waivered, even in his nineties – new technology didn't daunt him and he mastered the latest photocopiers with minimum tuition. He even had a computer at home when he was in his late eighties, something I wouldn't fancy. A great bloke and somebody I always had time and respect for.

DORIS HOOPER
née Reeve

Doris, eighty-eight, doesn't have a television. She's never had a television.

It's never appealed to me, I think it's a timewaster. I like crosswords, sewing, knitting and listening to the radio or CDs. TV is just a big black box in the corner to me.

I grew up in Dutton Lane and lived there until the age of twenty-six. One row of houses was privately owned and rented out and our row belonged to the railway who allocated these to railway firemen. My dad was a maintenance electrician and could be called to work at any time, so we had no. 13. I suppose no one else wanted it! It wasn't particularly unlucky for us.

The road was gravel and cows from the farm would come up and down twice a day to graze on the fields. These fields flooded every year which made better grass for the cattle. When the water drained away flowers (such as king-cups and milk-maids) quickly sprung up. On a drier field behind there'd be a spread of cornflowers and buttercups, it was a very pretty and colourful sight.

During summer holidays all the children would go off with sandwiches and a bottle of pop made from lemonade powder. The fields at the top of the lane were our playground. A tiny stream came off the main river and on a hot day we would sit there to cool off. When we finished playing, the girls would pick cornflowers and different grasses, making posies to take home to their mums. We did have a lovely time, we were free and would arrive home very tired and ready for bed.

Before we knew it, time came to get a job. Working class girls had little choice; it was either in service, on the factory floor or behind a shop-counter. I decided shop work was better than the other two. My mother put my name

Doris Hooper.

down at Wards, the drapers in the High Street while I was still at school. At fourteen, I was in that long dark shop selling all sorts of things. For window dressing, Mr Ward hung lots of strings down from the ceiling, with little wooden rods attached to them. We laughingly called them 'bird perches'. He would display socks and other light items on them. It was all good experience as I moved on to the big Co-op store and received more wages than the other new girls – 7s 6d a week. The Co-op was brightly lit, well organised with attractive displays – I was happy there.

Then, of course the Second World War came, changing everybody's lives. I was very shy in those days and hated being among complete strangers. I knew that at eighteen, I'd be called up but the carriage works had contracts for aircraft and desperately needed women. So I volunteered to work for the railway where I knew people.

There was an apprentice called Alan who pulled my leg something awful as he sharpened tools, etc., for the engineers. We started going out in 1942. He wasn't fighting in the war because he was in an essential job. Alan was

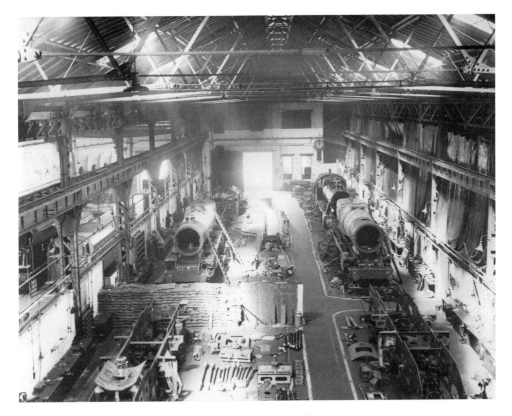

Inside the railway works. (Hampshire Museums and Archives)

also a good pianist. There was a shortage of pianists in the town with so many men away, so he spent a lot of evenings playing for the town hall dances. He saved this extra money to buy a motorbike with a sidecar and we considered ourselves very lucky.

On 3 June 1944 we married and travelled to near Blackpool for our honeymoon. Returning home, the D-Day invasion was over, there'd been no action related to this up north but here, down on the south coast, Mum said the roads and skies were crowded with military vehicles and planes.

I moved across the road from my parents to my Granddad's, where Alan and I lived in rooms. Our rent money must have been useful to Granddad. People said he was miserable but he had a lot to be grumpy about. He came from Devon and worked as a porter on the railway there. When he was nineteen, however, he somehow slipped (I'm not sure of all the details but he lost both legs – one above the knee and one below). He was courting my grandma at the time and said if she didn't stick by him he wouldn't bother to pull through. She didn't desert him, he learned to walk again on wooden legs and eventually they married, having two sons. After the accident, the railway said he could either have compensation or a job for life. He decided on the job for life and was sent to Eastleigh where he retrained to be a tinsmith. He made the little lamps they had on front of the steam trains. I think he sat down and they brought him all the parts. He walked to work from Dutton Lane. If it snowed he couldn't get home and they'd bring him back in a wheelbarrow! I can remember him asking my Dad to come across and file a bit of wood off because it was digging into his skin. When it was very hot, he'd swell up and couldn't even get his legs off, he'd have to sleep in them. However, he worked until retirement age and lived to be ninety.

I waited for six years after marriage and had two children before we got a home of our own. The council offered us a house in Nightingale Avenue.

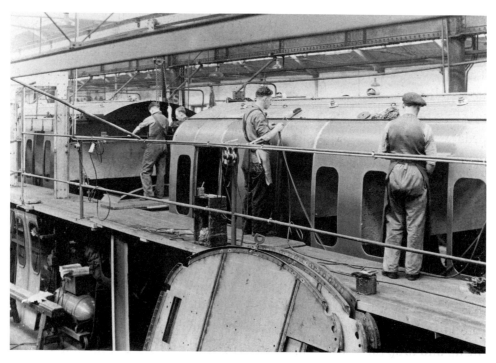

Men working on carriage construction. (Hampshire Museums and Archives)

The rent was £1 5s a week and we didn't know how we could afford it – we'd only been paying 11s to Granddad.

We had so little to bring here that Alan removed the sidecar from the motorbike and put planks of wood on, securing our belongings on top with a rope. We couldn't afford much furniture but gradually got our home kitted out. We managed.

In Dutton Lane the terraced houses had long passages which were decorated very dark. Our brand new home was beautiful. All the rooms were painted in cream, so light and airy and cheerful. It was so spacious, we couldn't believe our luck.

Sixty-one years I've been here. That first day we'd not had time to eat so were pleased to see a fish and chip van stop outside. We sat on the stairs tucking into our cod and chips – a happy memory and I still love my fish and chips!

Nightingale Avenue was a gravel road in 1950 and we had to walk to Passfield Avenue for a bus. It's a long road, especially as we're right up at the Chestnut Avenue end (which was just a lane then).

* * *

Twenty years later Alan died of mesothelioma. An awful disease. I believe he was the first asbestos case from the works. What hit me so hard was the fact that he never smoked or drank, would run everywhere and cycle to work, pedal home for his dinner and back again. He was a very fit man and coming down like that, it's cruel, it really is. He was only forty-eight.

Those following years were particularly sad for me. There'd been Alan, my two children, and my nephew living here. In a very short time, the youngsters married and moved out and then my husband died. Down from five to one, I was left alone in the house and it was awful, really awful. I'd always been a dancer and my friends would encourage me to go back dancing but I didn't feel I should. They kept saying to me, 'It would be good for you, help you get over it,' which it did do. They were so kind to me, saying, 'We're going to so-and-so dance on Saturday, Doris, d'you want to come with us?' They'd pick me up and drop me back again. Friends really helped me during that difficult period.

I kept my dancing going until I was seventy-eight, and I did all the digging in the garden – I gave it a good heavy digging, not just turning the top over. My garden was my pride and joy, I grew raspberries, strawberries, blackcurrants – all sorts. I carried on until I found I was giving them all away yet nobody was giving me anything. People used to swap years ago. Gradually I gave up, and I couldn't bend down to pick the strawberries anymore, owing to problems with my knees.

I like being independent but never walk further than I know I can return. Once a week I get a lift to Age Concern lunch club and stay on to watch the others dance – the music and company is always enjoyable. It was me who started these clubs seven years ago, and membership has grown. I'm still dinner money and subs monitor, handwriting the accounts in a hardback notebook, without a calculator.

Dial-A-Ride collect me once a fortnight to go shopping. They're marvellous and do things like carry your shopping into your kitchen for you; that's a great help. Alternate weeks I arrange a Dial-A-Ride trip into the centre. My daughter insists I get out and you do meet people, sitting at the bus stop.

I don't think young people mix with the older folk as they used to. I've a family with lovely children next door, but they never really stop to speak. Perhaps people haven't the time today, I don't know what it is. Years ago, we'd sit out in the bottom of our gardens in the summer, chat and make tea for each other. All the original residents were around the same age; we moved in at the same time and reared children who grew up together. That makes a community, I think.

But I'm happy, keep myself busy. Certainly don't feel the need for a television.

VERA SMITH
née Bendall

We moved to Bishopstoke from Shirley, Southampton, in 1954. I remember thinking that Eastleigh people had a different accent as many railway people came from families who were originally Londoners. We bought a two-bedroom bungalow in Horton Way for £1,750, paying a deposit of £80. Six years later we moved here to Whalesmead Road, which cost £2,250. There were no shops nearby then, but fifty-one happy years I've been here.

Vera, standing at the back, in front of Girls' Brigade banner, with ladies from Eastleigh Floral Society, November 1988. (Vera Smith)

A lot of people in Eastleigh town moved out to places like Fair Oak and Chandler's Ford because they wanted new houses. The redbrick terraces seemed old-fashioned then, but now people like what they call 'period' features.

I didn't go out to work until my daughter was fifteen and my son ten. I went to Lyons Bakery where Heinz Burt of pop music fame worked alongside me. He had shaky hands and we thought it was to do with the pop world lifestyle. We felt so guilty when we discovered he had Motor Neurone Disease, which he died of in 2000. He would ask the women if they had any annuals – *Bunty*, etc. – containing articles of when he was famous for his wife to see. My daughter had some in the attic so I gave them to him.

I'm eighty-five and still go swimming at Fleming Park. My friend and I always swam twenty lengths, but now we can only manage sixteen. I pop into Eastleigh three times a week to browse around the shops and have a cup of tea. I like to get out and see people.

NORA GOUGH
née Cooper

I've lived here in Chamberlayne Road ever since I was a baby. My mother died when I was eleven months old so my grandparents brought me up. Eastleigh has really grown over the years; I'm nearly eighty-five so have seen a lot of changes. The northern end of Leigh Road was all fields and, because people didn't have cars, Sunday afternoons were family walk times when I was a child. We'd walk to Swaythling, Bassett, all sorts of places.

There wasn't much money about. Most people worked for the railway, so the town was lucky to have those jobs. At noon the hooter blasted and soon Grantham Road was full of men cycling home for their hot dinners. The hooter also sounded in the morning; they had to start at seven and if they were five minutes late they had their wages docked.

My first memory is from when I was three about a lady in Wilmer Road who ran a little kindergarten. She earned a small living from this as she couldn't go out to work because her mother was an invalid. It was very modest but I loved it – she had crates, a bit like orange boxes, which we sat on while she told us a story, and later we'd turn them upside down and pretend we were in ships, or whatever you wanted it to be. They didn't have all this health and safety stuff in those days. The toilet was outside and round a corner. If it rained we used a chamber pot in the scullery. We didn't mind. But people now would be shocked.

I enjoyed the infants' school at Cranbury Road. Teachers organised little plays which everyone had to be in. These would also be put on at the town hall. I loved that as, like most little girls, I enjoyed dressing up.

There'd be maypole dancing on May Day at the Town Rec and at other times thick ropes hung from the pole, with big knots at the end which you could run with and then swing into the air.

Nora Gough aged 9, photographed at Cranbury Road School. (Nora Gough)

Best Wishes
XMAS 1935

I reckon parents sent their kids to the swimming pool over at Bishopstoke when they wanted them out of the way. Tuppence you paid, I think, and you could stay all day. We'd take jam sandwiches and a bottle of drink made with lemonade powder and you could sit on the grass which was always absolutely crowded with children. There was a shop that did a roaring trade. Although a lifeguard was on duty, people didn't worry if you couldn't swim, like me. I had a rubber tyre and I loved to stretch my feet onto the side, my arms clinging to the rubber ring and shoot backwards. One day I did that and the tyre came off. I wasn't quite out of my depth but deep enough and I remember all these bubbles when I was under the water. I couldn't get to the surface so put my hand out and grabbed hold of someone who shrugged me off. Eventually I righted myself but didn't learn to swim until I was twelve. I went to the High School (now Barton Peveril) who took pupils to the baths but only had one lesson because the war started. Luckily I got the hang of it.

I didn't even want to go for the scholarship. Gran took me along to take the exam, where we ten to eleven year olds sat in this huge hall on separate tables, seemingly miles apart. I didn't find the exam difficult, so passed, much to my surprise. We wore green pleated gymslips with a cream blouse which you had to buy from a special shop in Southampton. My grandparents were short of money, so we had a grant. That one gymslip, I was told, had to last me right through school. As you can imagine, you're a complete different size and shape by the time you're sixteen, but it lasted me out! Of course by that time the war had started and we had coupons for clothes.

I developed at twelve and my grandmother took me shopping for a bra, and also a corset, a big, heavy garment with lots of hooks and eyes. Eventually girdles and roll-ons became the norm but women wear as little as possible now.

In 1937, 4,000 Spanish children came over, refugees from the Spanish Civil War. My sister and I volunteered to help out at the camp in Chestnut Avenue. There were big triangular-shaped tents to sleep eight, with feet facing the middle. We helped fill the palliasses with straw and when the children actually arrived it was so exciting for us. We were all up there and apparently Gracie Fields visited them, though we didn't see her. They were supposed to be in quarantine when they first came but the older ones used to nip out and come through the woods. We communicated by sign language and it was quite something for Eastleigh to have all these foreign children. Eventually they were officially allowed to wander around and they would march down the road singing 'La Cucaracha'. We learned to sing along too.

They were moved to Rownhams all of a sudden so we tried to find them, though hadn't a clue where Rownhams was. We were aged ten, walking along near where Asda is now, when we were stopped by a policeman. He asked what

Basque children at the Chestnut Avenue campsite, 1937. (Basque Children Organisation)

we were doing and we said, 'Going to Rownhams to see the Spanish children.' He said 'You'd better get off home!' so we did as we were told.

The Second World War started and a bomb dropped on the mayor's house which was just down the road. He was dug out alive but his wife was killed. Because the house wasn't in use any more, my grandmother had that garden as an allotment. I remember a British plane crashing into a house in the next road, I believe it was carrying a load of pilots. A girl I knew lived in that house but she was out visiting her auntie at the time. Her parents were killed as the plane sliced into the top of the house and landed on the edge of the green. All the boys would try to get souvenirs – as a child you think its exciting, don't think of the sadness and people's loss. I was too young to really understand the war. During raids I went next door to use a young couple's Anderson shelter, while my Gran would go under the stairs here. I think the men hung around in the road and talked, while the women and children used the shelters and I remember the tunnels under the Rec.

I met my husband at a dance in Southampton Guildhall. You had to queue all the way round the building to get in as there were so many people in Southampton, what with all the sailors and the troops travelling through. I was watching girls in fashionable, fancy, slingback shoes which you couldn't get on rations. They obviously were friendly with sailors and I quite envied them, being a Land Girl. A tall man tapped me on the shoulder and asked me to dance, then said, 'Let's get a bite to eat at the buffet.' That wasn't very grand, what with food shortages, but at the end of the evening he walked me to Central station. He asked me for a date but as the train drew out I realised he didn't know my address, so I was hanging out of the window trying to shout it to him. He found me and later we married; over the next twenty years we had seven children.

Yes, I've lived in this house nearly all my life. I don't see myself moving, it's so handy for the doctor, pub, fish and chip shop, just five minutes' walk to town. And it's all flat.

DAVID BULL

My parents moved to Velmore Road, Chandler's Ford, from Highfield, Southampton, in 1933 when I was six. My father Charlie was a commercial traveller, selling carpets and ironmongery on wages of commission only. My mother, May, previously ran a guest house with her sister, so she took in paying guests, mainly chemists and physicists at Pirelli General. These earnings helped my brother Dick and I attend grammar school.

Our family attended Chandler's Ford Congregational Church where my father was an elder. I still chuckle at the memory of when he sneezed enormously loudly while we listened to a serious sermon. It was such a strong sneeze that

Standing down of the Home Guard, Chestnut Avenue Battalion, August 1945. David Bull is back row, first on left. (David Bull)

his false teeth flew out and landed a distance up the aisle. Dad calmly strolled up to his dentures, popped them back into his mouth, and sat back in his pew as if nothing had happened, while Mum broke into a fit of giggles.

Secondary years began at Taunton's Grammar School, Southampton. In 1939 this school of 600 boys was evacuated to Bournemouth. After three different 'foster' homes in as many months, my parents decided to bring me back home where I attended Eastleigh County High School (now Barton Peveril College). This was a mixed gender school, a shock as I knew little about girls and didn't learn much more as we were kept well apart. It was strictly against the rules to be seen talking or walking with the opposite sex.

In 1940/41 many schooldays were spent in air raid shelters. Schooling became severely disrupted, especially during the Battle of Britain. Close to the school, machine guns rat-tat-tatted as bombs fell on to the airport and aircraft factory (now Ford). The boys would listen to the noise of Spitfires and Hurricanes flying over and once watched a German plane hurtling to the ground. Our family home in Velmore Road burst at the seams as relatives and neighbours sought refuge – an extra sixteen people.

There were two men who made a lasting impression on me during that time. One was Mr Arthur Ellman, the handicrafts teacher. He gave all of his pupils a good grounding in woodwork, metalwork, etc., and many became successful surveyors, architects and builders. Mr Ellman was the only teacher at the High School without a degree. He was a skilled tradesman who, in the 1930s recession, took a City & Guilds teaching course rather than be unemployed. His students achieved excellent results, yet the headmaster looked down on him. I made a tea trolley, wooden and three-tiered, in Mr Ellman's class and it's still in use today.

The other was Mr Kenworthy who, along with another man, set up a Sunday school and youth club at Dr Golding's Surgery in Bournemouth Road. A lively and interesting programme kept us youngsters engaged and Mr Kenworthy often took us camping.

Like many other boys, I was in the Army Cadet Force. In August 1943, our group had a tough week away at an army camp, apparently being trained for the D-Day invasion which was nine months away.

One thing we liked to do was to cycle around finding wreckage from German planes. In the playground we had a barter system of bits of metal and also live

David Bull with the tea trolley he made at school seventy years ago.

ammo – bullets and incendiary bombs. We'd have been in big trouble with the headmaster if he'd discovered our lethal swapsies!

Our schooling and experiences certainly trained us for good citizenship. Academic success isn't everything, yet saying that our fifth year class of 1943 surprised everyone by gaining many credits and distinctions in our School Certificate exams.

On leaving school, I took up a six-year apprenticeship as a quantity surveyor. Before qualifying I met Doreen Wilkins at All Saints' Church. Her family lived in Market Street and Mr Wilkins worked as a charge-hand in the Wagon Shop at the Railway Works. In 1952 Doreen and I married. This was three years after I'd started work with a building firm in Basingstoke, so we moved to a rented house there.

We never returned to live in Eastleigh, eventually settling in Southampton. I rejoined All Saints' Church, though, taking on many different responsible

Left: *Doreen Wilkins and sister Beryl as 'flower girls' in about 1937 at the Church of the Resurrection, also known as the Parish Church. Doreen (1932–2009) later became Mrs David Bull. Beryl married Basil Gillingham and they still live in Chestnut Avenue near Barton Peveril College. (David Bull)*

Below: *The wedding of Doreen and David Bull, 1952. The best man, seen with the bridesmaids, is brother Dick Bull who became Deputy Headmaster of Chamberlayne Road Boys' School in the 1960s. (David Bull)*

Local newspapers would report weddings in the finest details. (David Bull)

Reprinted from *The Eastleigh Weekly News, August 21st,* 1952

BIG CROWD AT WEDDING

CHURCH WORKERS MARRIED

Eastleigh Parish Church on Saturday was the scene of a wedding which aroused considerable interest. The contracting parties were Miss Doreen Alice Wilkins, youngest daughter of Mr. and Mrs. A. Wilkins, of 180, Market Street, and Mr. Alfred David Bull, eldest son of Mr. and Mrs. H. C. Bull, of 87, Chamberlayne Road. The bride and bridegroom are ardent church workers at All Saints' Church, Miss Wilkins as a Sunday School teacher and Mr. Bull as a senior server.

There were about 200 present at the church to witness the ceremony, which was performed by the Rev. David Kee, a former priest-in-charge at All Saints'. The bridal party was met at the church porch by the choir and servers, and preceded by the cross bearer, were led in procession to the singing of the hymn, "Praise, my soul, the King of Heaven," to the chancel.

The bride, who was given away by her father, churchwarden at All Saints', wore a gown of white figured taffeta, with train and embroidered veil held in place by her head-dress of flowers. Her shower bouquet was of pink carnations and fern.

She was attended by a matron of honour (Mrs. Beryl Gillingham) (sister), Miss Barbara Cole (friend) and little Miss June Boyce (cousin). The two elder attendants wore ankle-length gowns of gold taffeta with organdie over-dresses and head-dresses of roselandia roses and blue scabious. Miss Boyce, who also acted as train bearer, was attired in an ankle-length gown of pale green taffeta with organdie overdress, and her head-dress was also of roselandia roses and scabious. The two elder attendants had bouquets of roses and scabious and the younger a Victorian posy of the same flowers.

The duties of best man were carried out by Mr. Richard Bull (brother of the bridegroom).

FULLY CHORAL

Mr. J. R. A. Lowton was at the organ, and Messrs. A. Boyce, J. Horton, B. Kessell and E. Webster acted as ushers.

The service was fully choral, other hymns sung being "Father, hear the prayer we offer," "O perfect love" and "May the grace of God our Saviour," and the 67th psalm was chanted. During the signing of the register the full choir rendered Brother James' Air, and the happy couple left the church to the strains of Mendelssohn's Wedding March.

At the reception held at the Parish Hall 110 guests assembled and the beautiful three-tier wedding cake was cut. Fifteen telegrams and four congratulatory cards were received, including one telegram from the Old Bartonians' football club, of which the bridegroom is an active member. A toast to the bride and bridegroom was proposed by the bride's father and received with acclamation, and the health of the bridesmaids was proposed by the bridegroom. Mr. C. Cole proposed a toast to the bride's parents and voiced the thanks of the company to them.

MANY PRESENTS

Among the hundred or more valuable and useful presents received by Mr. and Mrs. Bull was a substantial cheque from Messrs. G. W. Oliver and Sons, Ltd., builders, of Basingstoke, by whom the bridegroom is employed, and a glass fruit bowl and stand from the servers at All Saints'. The bride was the recipient of a dinner service from her colleagues at the Inland Revenue Office at Southampton and an oak biscuit barrel from the Sunday School teachers. They also received gifts from the Lincoln Club and other church organisations with which they are connected.

The honeymoon is being spent at Teignmouth, South Devon, the bride travelling in a two-piece in deep rose pink with matching hat and grey bird's-eye check coat and black accessories. On their return they will take up residence at Basingstoke.

Music at the reception was provided by Mrs. Smith, and during the evening ices were served.

roles. Church life is important to our families. Working at a youth club was one of my interests and I spent much time at Eastleigh's Centre 66 and setting up a youth hostel. That was rewarding, some youngsters had difficult problems at home.

I've had a wonderful life with happy memories of my childhood. I often visit Eastleigh and love browsing around the museum before indulging in a slice of home-made cake and cup of tea in the café there.

BERYL ANDREWS
née Banks

Beryl, of Chandler's Ford, talks about her parents' shop in wartime Bishopstoke.

We moved to Bishopstoke from Yorkshire in 1939 when I was twelve. My parents, Ernest and Olive Banks, ran a corner shop in Church Road. It was hard work, open all hours and of course with Second World War rationing there was a points system. I helped out at weekends. People don't realise how much work went on behind the scenes when the shop door closed. Everyone had a book full of different coloured tiny coupons as some things weren't rationed but were worth so many points, such as a tin of pineapple. Supplies were limited but there was a choice within that shortage. People had to register at the shop where they would obtain their basic rationed goods.

Understandably, people thought if you had a shop you were OK and didn't go short but believe me that wasn't so. Sometimes supplies were limited and there was not enough to go round the registered customers. You had to juggle. For instance, if Mrs Smith had pineapple last month then it was Mrs Jones' turn. Some elderly people didn't understand the system and needed a lot of help. The points tokens were smaller than a postage stamp and you had to count them – very fiddly. I'd regularly go to the Food Office in Romsey Road as all collected coupons had to be checked. They made sure you weren't cheating and if you'd made a mistake, you received a stern black look. Then I'd go to Ingrams, the tobacconists near Woolworths, to collect any cigarettes that were available. Most adults smoked then, they didn't realise the hazards. There was a bus stop outside our shop and the workmen

Staff of the Railway Accounts Office enjoy a works outing, 1949. (Hampshire Museums and Archives)

on their way to the carriage works would pop in before seven for their pack of five Woodbines to take to work.

We used to pat the butter on a slab (people were entitled to 2oz) and we had big rounds of cheese which you cut with a wire. In the summer it was very difficult to store food because there were no fridges in ordinary homes then.

On Sunday mornings I washed the shop floor. For blackouts we had steel shutters made to fit around the shop and it was my job to get those up and down. We did have some bombs drop nearby, but fortunately nobody was hurt. Once I was with a friend in the back room and we heard a bomb coming down so we threw ourselves down on the floor near the piano. We had those big sweet jars in the shop and not one of them cracked but further down on St Margaret's Road all of their windows shattered. We were nearer the incident but no damage. In the worst raids we would just go inside the cupboard under the stairs – a lot of good that would have done but that's what people used to do. A neighbour had a shelter but that became waterlogged. The infants' school in Church Road had shelters, so occasionally we would go there.

Sometimes water supplies were affected and my friend and I filled buckets from the standpipe in the road for some of the old people. There was definitely a camaraderie.

My parents kept the shop until 1948, by which time I'd been through Eastleigh County High School and had a job in the railway accounts office. Easier physically than the shop!

JOAN LILL
née Pay

In 1935 my father came to work as a civilian mechanic in the RAF Sheds, at what was then Stoneham Farm. I was six when we moved from Upavon in Wiltshire to Eastleigh where we all got dumped into Stanley Road. It had a bad reputation as the headmistress at Cranbury Road School tut-tutted, 'Oh dear, Stanley Road,' when my mother gave our address.

I enjoyed the move – Upavon had two pubs and only one shop while Eastleigh seemed to have a corner shop on every street and plenty to wander around in the town, just a short walk away. When the RAF held dances at the town hall, Mum and Dad managed the cloakrooms there. With no babysitter, I'd go along with them and remember watching graceful ladies in beautiful dance dresses waltzing, etc. I loved dancing and I also loved standing outside churches looking at weddings.

When the Second World War started, Dad was called up – at thirty-nine he was considered elderly! My mother worked in the carriage works as a fitter during the war. There wasn't a lot of money coming in, so I was a latchkey kid. I don't know much about Dad's war years because he wouldn't talk about it. His ship was torpedoed and he was badly injured, so spent a long time in Odstock hospital, where we visited him a lot.

One day when we lived in the High Street, Mum screamed at me from the garden, a German plane was plummeting down towards our street. Lower and lower it came until I could see the pilot's face. There was a barrage balloon on the playing fields where Eastleigh College is now and I believe the plane crashed into the ropes.

Schooling was disrupted because we were in air raid shelters a lot. We had an Anderson shelter in our garden and Mum, myself and our lodger

*Cranbury Road
Schools, 1900.*

slept in there most nights. I was disappointed not to pass the grammar scholarship and so went to Chamberlayne Road School where I learned shorthand-typing. When I left, I started clerical work in the accounts office in the railway carriage works, there were six of us school-leavers who started on the same day at 11s a week. It was very boring; we used big adding machines and had to work from nine until seven which is hard when you're fifteen. It messed up my evening activities: drama club, Guides, church events, so I was not too pleased. We had a strict supervisor whose desk was by the ladies' toilets. If she thought you'd spent too long in there, she would come and get you! She was a very glamorous woman, bright red lipstick and nail varnish; rumour had it she was having an affair with someone high up. On the whole, though, the railway was good to work for. We had outings, a social club and sport events – there was always cricket, football, tennis, etc.

Then I moved away as I wanted to be nearer the bright lights. My husband Dennis and I met working at Deepdene in Dorking and we married in 1959. My parents remained in Eastleigh and Dad eventually went to work for the railway and stayed there until he retired. In 1966 we moved back down, to Chandler's Ford, and are still in the same house. We like our neighbours.

I find myself going to Eastleigh more often as my daughter moved there. She had a baby recently so we walk the buggy around different roads. I was shocked to see my old junior school no longer existed, in its place was a block of flats. I passed our old house and thought 'oh dear, things change so much!'

MARION BRÉHAUT
née Hearn

Stanley Bréhaut set up his photography business when he came out of the army. His family were originally Channel Islanders, hence the surname, but Stan was born in Market Street over the pie shop and I came from Chadwick Road. We met when I was twenty and working in the Co-op. A friend was taking her little girl to be photographed and asked me to go with her. Stan and I just looked at each other and clicked. We discovered I had a natural flair for photography so we really did become a team. Then Stan became a cameraman for ITV, so while he worked in television I practically ran the business on my own.

We enjoyed the photography; we did it because we liked it. If we'd have been more businesslike we could probably have made a lot of money but that didn't interest us. You couldn't run a business like that now, you'd be out of pocket. It's cutthroat these days, although back then it was hard work too with long hours, but that was our choice.

When it came to carnival time we took it in turns: four hours in the darkroom while the other grabbed four hours' sleep. That was every night throughout the week. The first year we did it was in the 1950s and we had all the photographs in the windows by morning when the men would be walking or cycling past on their way to the rail works. Word got about and afterwards it was expected we'd do it every year.

The streets would be absolutely thronged with people for the carnival; they'd be up on the park, and partied until quite late at night. The Stevens Fair always came that week. Thinking about it, the war hadn't been over that long and it was something people could get together on. The carnival would line up on Passfield Avenue, from near the corner of Leigh Road and

Stan and Marion Bréhaut outside their shop, June 1953. (Marion Bréhaut)

Men returning to rail works.

down to Derby Road. That's a long line of floats, half a mile. The route was down Derby Road and into the town. Stan and I would go by motorbike taking all the shots. I can still see us riding down Derby Road – no crash helmets as people just didn't wear them then. It was a disaster waiting to happen really. Everyone would cheer as we scooted by because they all knew us and our job. Then it was straight back to the darkroom and processing the reels and reels. The first carnival was in 1887 and I think its heyday was in the 1950s and '60s. Once the railway, Caustons and Pirellis petered out, it became smaller.

Carnival aside, we did mainly weddings and baby portraits. There was a clinic nearby in Chamberlayne Road so the mums strolled pass pushing prams and on the way back made an appointment to have photographs taken.

Stan also played in a dance band – three dance bands in fact. He was into Hawaiian guitar music. I also worked for the *Eastleigh Weekly News*, going out and about with Frank Brown, the reporter. Sometimes I worked for the *Echo*. However, I was badly injured in a car crash and had to pack it up – I was hit by a car that crossed the central reservation and was in a wheelchair for a long time.

Stan and I had fifty-four happy years together. He died in hospital in 2005. I'm eighty now and people say you get used to widowhood. But that hasn't happened for me.

GEORGE CLEMENTS

I'm the only original owner left in Glebe Court, Fair Oak. My wife Patricia and I bought this bungalow in 1962, brand new, helped by her father generously loaning us the deposit. The purchase price was £3,250 and a mortgage commitment seemed a huge undertaking then (my parents always rented).

I was born in 1937 at no. 14 Shaftesbury Road. Mum was one of nine, a local girl while Dad came from Kennington, London. I was an only child; Dad took his first look at me in the nurse's arms and said that one's enough! At five, I went to Shaftesbury Road School which was next to Boyatt Wood. And it was a wood then, we enjoyed playing there.

There was a dear old chap in no. 30 who would stand at his gate and say 'Hullo son, come by lunchtime and I'll have some conkers for you.' He had a horse chestnut tree and saved them for you. Sadly, a man doing that now would be regarded as very suspicious!

Every Saturday a Mr Jones collected our insurance money. He rode a bike but had a gammy leg and could only move the good leg to pedal. Another lady came round and collected a few bob so that you could see the doctor if you were ill. This was called the Doctors Club. Our payment book would always be on the shelf by the front door. People called, collected or delivered which was very sociable. I loved telling Mum who was at the door.

Opposite our house was the old Council Depot. From our front room, you could tell the time because of the clock on that building. Further up was a long corrugated iron fence and we kids loved to run alongside it with a stick. This made a noise like a machine gun and any grown up nearby would tell us off.

We were near to Byron Road, the site of the local Harris bacon factory. Some houses in Shakespeare Road belonged to this company which let them out to employees. All day long lorries containing pigs on their way to the slaughterhouse would go by. Those poor animals seemed to know their fate the way they squealed so loud – terrifying noise it was. Another sound I remember is being in bed, trying to get to sleep, but you'd hear a constant muffled thump, thump, thump. Dad told me it was a drop hammer from the metal presses at the locomotive works.

In Consort Road was a pickle factory where the owner handed out sacks of onions to people who peeled them for some extra money. A lady near our house did this and the smell used to waft everywhere, it was horrible. Her eyes must have really stung and her house stank.

Of course, most people have heard of Hanns Dorset Dairies because of Benny Hill. My Dad worked there for a while, mucking out the stables and looking after the horses. The milkmen would arrive at the dairy at 4.30 a.m. to get their horses and carts sorted out. My dad had several jobs; he had to get what he could to keep us going.

Like most Eastleigh people of my age, I've fond memories of Hillickers in the High Street, a pease pudding and faggot shop. You'd take your own basin for the gravy to be poured into. Very tasty, this was a pay-day treat.

Also in Consort Road was what we called 'the Balley Hole', a huge pit where ballast was dug out from. People chucked all sorts of junk in that. I wanted a bike but there was no money for one so I went to the Balley Hole and found a frame, then came across some handlebars – gradually I built my own bike. I couldn't afford any inner tubes so I stuffed the tyres with dried grass – puncture-proof tyres!

As a nipper I was fascinated by anything mechanical or electrical. I liked to make my own crystal radio sets. I loved to pop into the Brice Slade radio shop where Mr Brice would show me tips in building these. I was indebted to that man for being so patient and helpful and I'm still interested in vintage wireless and the old programmes.

Not everyone had wireless sets and Eastleigh Radio Relay Exchange provided a rental service with wires running to their customers' houses, where there'd be a little wooden box in the living room. This was a speaker with a knob you could turn to receive four radio stations: the Home Service, Third Service, The Light Programme and Luxembourg.

In 1952, before I left school, my father and I went to see Mr Cox of the Nalder Cox electrical shop at 20 High Street. He offered me a job and I started off as dogsbody; making tea, getting the engineers' lunch from the bakers, mending irons, toasters and fires, tinkering with radio sets, sometimes serving in the shop. I used to charge radio accumulators (an accumulator was a square glass jar containing acid with lead plates). The acid was very corrosive so you had to be very careful.

If a house was not on electricity, to power a wireless you needed three things: firstly a 100v dry cell battery which was quite expensive but lasted a long time, a smaller battery called a grid bias and an accumulator for ordinary power and that had to be taken into a shop to be recharged. You had two of these, one with the radio being used and another to take in for recharging. I think the charge was 6d.

One of the engineers taught me to drive in the Ford van, then I was sent out in the thick of it on my own. Televisions were gradually appearing in people's homes, so I delivered, put up aerials, fixed simple things or otherwise brought the set back. I was given day release at the university, to qualify as a television engineer and then took evening classes to receive my certificate. There was no tech college then.

Only posh people in places like Chilworth and Chandler's Ford could afford a television set. They would impress the neighbours with an invitation to coffee evenings where people watched in the dark because the picture wasn't that bright. It still makes me laugh thinking about the picture reception in those days, it was awful! Some nights you'd be watching a snow storm on the screen, which were always 9in or 12in.

At twenty-one years old, I was offered a job at DER in St Mary Street, Southampton, as a service engineer. While working there I met my wife, Patricia, who came from Swaythling. You never know what might happen in the day of a TV engineer! Once I couldn't fix a customer's telly and he was desperate to see a big football match. I told him the set was unfixable, he'd need another one. As I walked down his garden path, he shouted and swore before throwing the set at me! Luckily it missed but I can still see it, smashed to smithereens all over his garden.

After colour TVs became the norm, I couldn't face more training so took the plunge and worked for myself, doing home electrical work. The first time I saw a fridge was when I was sent out as an apprentice to the

The prefab homes at 'the Hundred', c. 1947. (Eastleigh Borough Council)

'Hundred', an area between Chestnut Avenue and Arnold Road, where 100 pre-fab bungalows were built after the war. Apparently the council equipped them with fridges. These temporary homes existed long after their expected sell-by date. They were cosy and well-planned, the occupiers loved them and many took pride in making their gardens look nice. I got to know a few people who lived there and they were sorry when the time came to move out.

There are some characters that stick in my mind and I mean 'characters' in the nicest sense of the word. Before the NHS you could go into Wainwrights the chemist in Market Street and ask for Mr Taylor. Everyone went there and said to the shop assistant, 'Excuse me can I see Mr Taylor?' He'd come out and you'd tell him your symptoms and he'd say, 'That's all right. I'll sort that out for you.' Then he mixed you up a bottle of medicine or put tablets into an envelope. People got better and saved money by not seeing a doctor – Mr Taylor was very highly respected.

And then there was Mr H.T. Torbock who owned the first supermarket locally. When I was a nipper, starting in the radio shop, Mr Torbock would

Torbock's shop, before 1950. (Hampshire Museums and Archives)

come out and talk to me. I thought, 'Isn't this nice, he's a big business man and he's got time to talk to someone like me.'

There was Nelson Mullins, the rag and bone man from Desborough Road. If you wanted any bits and pieces difficult to come by in the war, he'd do his best to find it for you. I think he had a horse and cart. The other Eastleigh rag and bone man certainly did. You'd hear him coming, clip-clop-clippity-clop, shouting 'Ol' Ragbone, Ol' Ragbone!'

Yes, it's strange what remains in your memory. Mum used to take me to the old Fleming Park recreational grounds. It had a pond in front of the entrance with a notice saying 'Not Mine, Not Thine, But Ours'. I like that.

DEREK DARLING

when people think of retirement in a new town, they may well decide on Worthing. Derek Darling, though, moved from Worthing to Eastleigh.

Our only daughter, Lisa, lived in Winchester and when her baby was on the way, she very much wanted us to move closer. That was thirteen years ago when we had a guest house in Worthing. We put it up for sale but by the time we sold it our new granddaughter was two years old! As usual, buying and selling is a stressful chicken-and-egg situation. Once we had a firm sale, we were desperate to find something suitable in Hampshire so Lisa discovered this house in Leigh Road.

'Dad,' she said, 'I've found it. The ideal house for you.'

'Where?' I asked

'Eastleigh.'

'Where?' I couldn't remember where Eastleigh was, though it turned out we'd been taken to The Point and the Swan Centre a few times. We came down, saw Leigh Road with its double yellow lines and the neglected state of the house for sale and thought 'oh, no.' However, there is an advantage to double yellow lines: no one else can park outside your gates either. There was a parking space and a garage at the rear in Dew Lane and the 90ft garden was south-facing. What's more, it was well within our price range. A local builder said that with all the dilapidated artex ceilings and walls plus the alterations we wanted, it would be best if everything was completely stripped back. Luckily, we were offered use of a flat in Winchester for six months while this work was carried out. We'd been disappointed we couldn't afford to buy in Winchester but once living there thought it was too hilly for people getting older like us. As beautiful as this cathedral city is, we found parking difficult and traffic very busy. We moved into Leigh Road and appreciated the benefits: bus stop outside, walking distance to the shops and amenities and it was flat! Also, there was closeness of the M27 and M3, trains to Waterloo and a regional airport. We like airports. Years ago we lived close to one in Shoreham and enjoyed plane spotting. That said, my wife Gillian finds planes here rather boring as they're mostly Fly Be. However, we do get a Spitfire on special occasions.

So there we were, 1990, and starting our retirement in Eastleigh. Another downside of our new home was the pebbledash, painted an awful pink, like a raspberry Chewit sweet. I remember chatting to the young teller at the bank, saying she'd see us often as we'd moved in

'Whereabouts?' she asked.

'Leigh Road.'

'Not the pink house?'

'Yes. But it won't be pink for long. We're painting it cream.'

'Thank goodness for that,' she laughed.

A few weeks later we heard a knock on the door. A man introduced himself as Mike Buckingham, from across the road, an ex-Mayor of Eastleigh. I thought, 'So? You trying to impress me?'

He welcomed me to the town then went on to tell me about his chrysanthemums. He belonged to a Chrysanthemum Growers Club and often won prizes. I wasn't sure why he was telling me all this, apart from being neighbourly.

'I'm very pleased you're here and have done the place up,' he said, 'but I've one complaint.' I was puzzled. He continued, 'You've painted the house. Whenever I had a growers' meeting at my house, I could easily say to people "Look out for the pink house and I'm directly opposite."'

We laughed and have since become good friends. He'd always shower us with beautiful chrysanths but sadly his growers club no longer exists; older members have passed on and younger people aren't interested. He doesn't grow them anymore.

My wife joined Boyatt Wood WI and we wanted an outside interest that would include both of us, so we joined the Friends of Eastleigh Museum. Not long after, I was coerced into joining the committee, then one day found myself president! We've around thirty members, all of them in their later years. It's a shame younger people don't come along or perhaps that too will become extinct one day – I wonder if today's youngsters will only want to find

Eastleigh Museum, High Street, 2011.

Tableau inside the museum – a typical railway family's sitting room in the 1930s. (Photograph taken with permission from Eastleigh Museum)

Tableau inside the museum – a typical scullery in the 1930s. (Photograph taken with permission from Eastleigh Museum)

out about history on the internet and not talk to people. Modern technology just doesn't interest me; I like to hear people's voices, see their faces, have a proper conversation.

Retirement in Eastleigh has been happy, though Gillian was most upset when Littlewoods store disappeared from the Swan Centre. I've noticed a lot of shops disappearing. Like towns everywhere, it seems strange without a Woolworths – these days it's all estate agents, fast food takeaways and charity shops (in fairness we quite like looking in the charity shops). Since the council installed parking meters it's noticeable how the footfall in Eastleigh shops has decreased. The market has fewer stalls too. People used to drive in to shop here but now with the parking charges they don't bother. It's sad to see shops become boarded up, as it is with the pubs. I can think of at least two that have closed. Is it the recession or a change in younger people's lifestyles? They seem to prefer to buy drink from the supermarkets to have indoors in front of Facebook.

I'm certainly not a grumpy old man. Quite cheerful. We love going to the theatre and cinema, with The Point just down the road we consider ourselves lucky. We're very content, relaxing in our garden. We don't notice the Leigh Road traffic with the double glazing and we enjoy our conservatory at the back. We've made plenty of new friends and would not wish to return to Brighton where Gillian and I were born and bred. Nor Worthing. And Eastleigh does not feel like a retirement town full of silver surfers, it's a pleasure to see young mums walking past pushing their buggies and of course, we have the reason we moved here – our granddaughter – who no longer needs a babysitter. She comes to stay with us now, goes straight to her Nan's laptop and tries to persuade me to tap away. I'd rather mow the lawn.

MARY WEST
née Purchase

In 1907 my grandparents moved into 142 Cranbury Road where my father was born in 1908. When he had a family of his own, we lived there too. The houses were demolished to make way for a block of flats in 1963. I was twenty-seven then and living with my mother-in-law. A vivid picture remains in my mind of the day we were pushing my baby daughter in her pram past no. 142 just as the bulldozer ploughed into my old bedroom. You could see the wallpaper and other personal memories – I stood on the pavement and cried.

My grandfather was a postman for many years and my father went to school locally then married my mother. For a short while we lived in no. 136, three doors away, but granddad died when I was five so the family returned to be with grandma. I was very lucky with schools. I went to Cranbury Road Girls' School then passed my 11+ and went to Eastleigh County High School, which was then the other side of the block we lived in. My brothers went to Chamberlayne Road Boys' School, so we could pop round to school in no time at all.

Dad worked in the railway and was in the Home Guard (his eyesight wasn't good enough for the army). During the war my mother worked at the running sheds. Because she was employed by the railway she was allowed a special price for good quality two-course meals at the British Restaurant (a site now occupied by Sainsbury's), a nationwide firm. I often met mum at 2 p.m. and we'd enjoy a meal out.

VE Day was celebrated with a street party plus a party in the hall which is now an annexe to Eastleigh College. An elderly lady was all dressed in union jacks and our dog wore a red, white and blue bow. Cranbury Road was full of our relatives; so life was always very sociable.

I remember rationing and that some girls at school had pretty dresses, either in a subdued airforce blue or pale pink. I dearly wanted a pink one and discovered these girls had been to a place, something like the WVS, where you took old clothing and in exchange they gave you one of these dresses. I persuaded Mum to let me do this. I was so chuffed but the first day I wore it I came out in a dreadful rash as if I had the measles – absolutely smothered I was – so could never wear it again.

I left High School at fifteen because of health problems. I'd suffered badly from arthritis since I was seven, then by thirteen had tonsillitis once a month. With so much schooling missed, I didn't want to stay so my mother asked permission from Winchester to let me leave. I worked as a cashier at Storrs department store in Market Street, sitting in a little room upstairs where those metal cash containers would be sent, via an overhead cable. I'd put the change in and send it back, sort out receipts, etc. I'd also do a bit of mending and ironing for the man who did the shop windows. Then I had really bad arthritis and couldn't work for a while. My mother had the offer of her old job at Manor Bakeries, which was then Prices, and she worked on the big slab ovens. I stayed at home and did the housework and cooking, took my younger brother to school. A year later I started at Russells, the shoe people, who sent me to London for a Clarks' shoe fitting course. While working at Russells I met my husband, Derek West, who was brought up in Chadwick Road at the back of Pirelli's. It turned out his mother had been a postwoman and knew my granddad. She was more than keen for us to marry! Neither of us had much money as he was still an apprentice at the railway, so I got a job at Caustons making bank cheques. Derek's parents moved to Nutbeem Road and we lived with them. I was twenty when I married; he was a month off his twentieth birthday. There was friction between him and his mother, she was very domineering so we looked around for somewhere else.

We only went across to Derby Road, we could see each others' houses! We had rooms with a widower who spent weekends with his sister in Portsmouth. He was keen to give this house up but didn't want to put us out on the streets.

Caustons, 1930s. (Hampshire Museums and Archives)

People working in Caustons, 1980s. (Hampshire Museums and Archives)

When we were allotted a council house, I asked the council if we could stay where we were, after explaining the situation to them. So that's what happened. We'd been paying the rent anyway as our 'landlord' was a bad payer and inclined to get into debt. I think the council were pleased too. We lived in that house for thirteen years, then moved round to Burns Road. We never thought we'd be able to afford my dream home, a bungalow in Bishopstoke, but we managed it by our retirement.

Sadly Derek died soon after – he didn't have a long retirement. For the first six months there were many forms and practicalities to sort out. We'd done everything together, I felt so lost and found too much time and quiet on my hands.

The British Guild of Patchwork Quilters gave a talk at Eastleigh Museum, where I'd worked. I've always liked doing crafts so decided to take quilting up – I'd need something to occupy me in the winter nights. Now I go to all sorts of quilting shows and conferences, including three trips to America and one to Alaska. I belong to Southampton Quilters, held at Hedge End.

Mary West holding a hand-stitched Memory Quilt of her late husband.

Derek was into woodcarving, self taught, and my bungalow is decorated with a lot of his work, which was well thought of by professional carvers who said Derek could carve in 3D. That's very difficult. It's so lovely to have these mementoes of him.

Eastleigh Museum was my workplace for twelve years. It was an interesting job. When we were setting up the '1930s living room' tableau, we had great difficulty getting hold of a floral cross-over pinny for 'Mrs Brown' to wear. A customer overheard us and said, 'You want one of those old-fashioned pinnies? I've got a drawerful of my mother's. You're welcome to have them.'

I loved working there, especially when you showed schoolchildren around. They could never visualise what it was like during the war and because my childhood was in that era I could tell them how it was for local children then. They just couldn't believe people had newspaper for toilet roll, and continued using it well into the 1950s. That snippet would fascinate them and always raised lots of giggles.

I go into Eastleigh a few times a week, like to pop into the museum. I miss the old Eastleigh and the variety of shops we had. Now its just charity shops, estate agents and eating places – I'd much rather visit little villages. I belong to a lot of things besides the quilters so life is busy socially. I think that's good for you.

PAT BORG

My mother moved here from London when she remarried. Her new husband was an Eastleigh man and although I wanted to be near my Mum, I'd never considered leaving London. I had plenty of friends and interesting places to go to. But before Christmas, my brother and I followed, starting our new life in Sheers Road, Bishopstoke. It was 1959; I was twenty-one.

Eastleigh was obviously much quieter, more laid back than London. There didn't seem to be much to do and I didn't want to stay. Not being rude, but people weren't so friendly and appeared aloof towards strangers. However, Mum said 'Give it a few months, get yourself a temporary job.'

So I did. And that January, working on the finishing floor at Warner Lamberts in Chestnut Avenue, I met Joe who was in the warehouse and newly arrived from Malta. We married in the August. People said, 'It's far too soon to marry. You don't know anything about him. For all you know he could have a wife and children back in Malta.'

But here we are, fifty-one years later, still enjoying life together. I'll always remember our first date – at the Picture House in Market Street to see *The Guns of Navarone*. Once I met Joe I never hankered for London. We bought a house in Chandler's Ford and raised our two daughters – they both married Eastleigh boys.

I've seen a lot of changes since moving here. Eastleigh was busier then because of the railway works. The station was small and the big Railway Hotel next to it disappeared into a car park. Gone are all those little High Street shops like Liptons and the haberdashery – the list goes on and on. There was no motorway, just the Chandler's Ford bypass – I remember lots of fields with horses in.

Lots of changes have been for the good. I think Eastleigh Borough is a pleasant place to live. They say the crime rate is low and I never thought we'd

Pat Borg providing refreshments at the Age Concern club.

be here this long, let alone retiring here. Life is busy as we've always been involved with the local Lions, a charity organisation, and I do voluntary work for Age Concern. This belongs to the 'Fit As A Fiddle Scheme', which runs across the south. In our Romsey Road premises we have weekly tai-chi, curling, a lunch club and sequence dancing. Also, there is a cooking session for men who are on their own. A young nutrition expert teaches this but we're limited to quick recipes as we've only ninety minutes. Once we cooked a fish dish but no-one liked it as we couldn't get rid of the smell! The whole building reeked. I do enjoy my work at Age Concern. People are very appreciative. There's a lot of laughter, especially when we're talking at cross-purposes because someone is hard of hearing.

There's plenty going on for the elderly in Eastleigh. The Baptist church puts on meals, outings and a coffee morning every day for all ages, and the Methodist church organises similar events. No-one needs to be alone, the authorities have made good facilities for the elderly and lots of retirement apartments have sprung up. Think of what I'd have missed if I had not taken my mother's advice!

COLE MATHIESON

The Concorde Club moved to Stoneham Lane in 1970. Back in September 1957 I launched it as a jazz club at the Bassett Hotel, Southampton, but the end of the 1960s saw pubs becoming Berni or Schooner Inns, with food as the main priority, not music.

I realised I had no security of tenure at the Bassett Hotel. The club was thriving yet the thought of buying my own premises petrified me. I'd need to take out a huge bank loan and when a good friend, Roland Tucker, gave me the sale particulars of a derelict school near Eastleigh, I never imagined it becoming what it is today. Luckily Roland had vision, he saw way beyond two dilapidated buildings which had been empty for years, located on a narrow country lane.

'It's worth going for,' he said, 'especially as there's two acres of land.' The asking price was £7,250 – well above my means. No thanks. Then the Bassett gave me six months' notice to move out because of brewery modernisation. Out of the drawer, I retrieved the details of the North Stoneham school. The previous owner was Prices Bakery who used it as a sports and social club, so no need to apply for change of usage. Thus began a time of seeing bank managers, signing on the dotted line then physically getting into serious DIY. Luckily an army of helpers all rolled their sleeves up to tidy the buildings and grounds.

We've been adding bits on ever since. About eleven years ago we built the hotel, Ellington Lodge, and also expanded to events other than jazz – conferences, weddings, quiz nights – all sorts.

Music has always been a passion. I was brought up in a rented terraced house in Newtown, Southampton, and left the secondary modern, where I'd been a bit of a dummy, at fifteen. In my younger days I played drums in different bands, but I have to say, played badly. My talent, I discovered, lay in promoting. Jazz was a genre I fell in love with at the age of twelve, so was driven to hear and give opportunities to jazz bands. I've a wide appreciation of all types of jazz although some of the styles after 1970 don't appeal too much. Jazz comes and goes, people assume it's only for the older crowd. There are so many young musicians, especially with the number of music colleges available now, and they have jazz courses. Years ago there was only one. I think in the future a lot more young people will be interested in jazz because of the number of their contemporaries playing it. Jamie Cullum was a regular and popular performer here before he hit the big time. I've kept the jazz alive at the Concorde. We have two nights in the small room and two nights in the large venue.

My son Jamie joined us about eight years ago and he's developed the tribute band nights which are extremely popular. I seem to spend more time in the office as we're busy all year round and not just at night. There are organisations that have coffee mornings, lunches, fashion shows.

Retirement isn't something you think about in the music business, you just carry on until you drop. The Concorde has become a family concern with my son and one daughter working here as well as my wife. We've around thirty to forty permanent staff, many part-time.

I've met and become friends with so many amazing musicians, Humphrey Lyttelton in particular. He very kindly wrote an introduction to my book *The*

Derelict village school surrounded by weeds, 1969. (Concorde Club)

Cole Mathieson, renovation time, 1970. (Concorde Club)

Concorde Club – The First Fifty Years. Sadly he died the day the book went to the printers.

Things run fairly smoothly here. In the early days at the Bassett there'd be disasters with bands not turning up. Musicians travelled in battered unreliable vans then and often broke down miles away from a public phone box, but communication is so much easier these days.

Our audience covers a wide range of ages. We still get people from the Bassett days and younger people because of the tribute bands. On a Friday

Cole Mathieson chats with Humphrey Lyttelton. (Concorde Club)

The Concorde Club, 2011.

night, we'll have an older crowd in the Moldy Fig and youngsters bouncing around in the other room. Buddy Greco recently was tremendous and we book what are probably the finest big bands in Britain, one example is the Back to Basie Band. We've also had the London Community Gospel Choir – I really enjoyed them.

When we moved here, Eastleigh was definitely thought of as the other side of the tracks. I wouldn't put it on my address until the Postmaster General in Southampton wrote insisting that unless I put Eastleigh on our letterheads so people replied to the correct location, I wouldn't be receiving any post. But now, I think it is an advantage being in Eastleigh. What a lot of tremendous changes have happened over the years. The Borough Council takes in a big diverse area, yet there's a homely feel to the place.

There is always the future to plan for and we'd love to extend our 65-bedroom hotel by as much again. It's working well and makes a good package for our customers. When I think of the procession of bank managers we saw back in 1969 who laughed at our application, I still have a chuckle. NatWest was the first I tried. They told me, 'There is no way a club will succeed down that obscure country lane!'

MAVIS VERNON
née Miller

My grandparents came from Portsmouth where Granddad managed Fletchers, a butchery business. He moved here to start a new shop in Leigh Road as Eastleigh was expanding rapidly at the end of the nineteenth century. Some years down the line, there was a dispute so he set up his own butchers shop, Millers, in the High Street. He had a pony and cart which were stabled in Barton Road and my father would do meat deliveries on his bicycle.

My grandmother had ten children who lived, my father being the youngest. He contracted measles at the age of three which resulted in mastoids and he lost his hearing. In those days he'd have been called deaf and dumb, but he'd already learned to speak. At some stage he was sent to Plymouth where he was taught to lip read – too well, we used to say, because he never missed any secret that you whispered to someone! As a young man, he couldn't find work but because of the war and able-bodied men joining the forces, Pirelli offered him a job. With money coming in, he and my mother were able to marry in 1941 and I came along in 1944. I tell my grandchildren I exist because of Hitler!

I was born at my grandmother's house, 86 Desborough Road. This was a three-bedroom house with two living rooms. My parents had a living room and one bedroom, which I slept in, and also my brother later. We all shared the kitchen. There was a little paved area by the back door, then a low brick wall. The soil there was absolutely black because that's where the chimney sweep would empty the soot. My grandmother grew the most beautiful lilies of the valley in that part of the garden. Built onto the back of the house was an outhouse which combined both lavatory and coalhole. When you sat on the loo you looked at a pile of coal. Why did those outside toilets always have ill-fitting doors? A big gap at both the bottom and the top made it very draughty.

As a small child I had whooping cough badly. To help to ease my chest as I lay in bed was a Wright's Coal Tar dispenser, a naked flame heating the coal tar so that its fumes wafted around the room. Once it caught fire and because I was so ill, I couldn't cry out! Luckily someone smelled the burning, ran upstairs and the fire brigade came and evacuated the house. Thankfully we escaped major damage.

Next door, at that time there was a little shop selling wool and underwear. It's now a Chinese takeaway. On the opposite corner diagonally was another little shop which had big jars of sweets in the window. Inside it had string going across and there were pegs holding up colouring books. This shop was run by a Miss Croucher and her brother. When I was about four, my grandmother sent me across the road to buy some kindling. She handed me half a crown, which was a lot of money in those days. There was a step up over the threshold and between this and the floorboard was a slight gap – guess where my half a crown went! Miss Croucher took me home because I was petrified about telling my parents. Many years later the shop was refurbished. Up came the floorboards near the threshold and there was my half crown, which Miss Croucher brought to no. 86 and handed back to my grandmother.

One of my uncles had no children of his own, so he sometimes bought me clothes. He once bought me a beautiful blue coat with a little fur collar on it. I was thrilled with this. Mum and I were stood outside the railway station waiting for a bus when one of those very sooty trains came in. My lovely coat and I were absolutely covered in black smuts so Mum was furious and went charging in to the stationmaster who gave her some compensation.

My mother loved the cinema. The Regal and the Picture House changed their shows halfway through the week, so she'd see one on Monday and another across the road on Tuesday. Wednesday was housework time, then she'd do both cinemas again on Thursday and Friday. I used to love playing usherette when I lived at Desborough Road. I'd shine a torch to guide my grandmother from the front room then up the stairs to which ever stair she was to sit on, then I'd go back down to the hall and perform for her!

Coronation time in Market Street, 1953. The Picture House can be seen in the centre of the photograph. (Len Harvell)

The old Fleming Park Pavilion and grounds. (Hampshire Museums and Archives)

In about 1949, we moved from Gran's to the Nissen huts at Belmont Road, Chandler's Ford. Those semi-circular tin buildings had been converted into temporary civilian accommodation. They were divided internally with a breeze block wall to make units: two bedrooms, living room, a coke stove for heating and a kitchen. Outside you had your coal bunker and lavatory (there was no bathroom). A nearby copse went down to Fleming Park so my friends and I would play out all day, roaming the woods, climbing trees. Childhood was idyllic. We learned so much about flowers and trees and would paddle in Monks Brook, carrying jam jars to catch tiddlers. Fleming Park then was just a wooden pavilion on a recreation ground. Alongside was the bowling club which my father and some uncles belonged to. When we were hungry we'd turn up to get fed! We were in the Nissen hut for about three years then Mum and Dad were allocated a council house at Monks Way.

I loved school, it was marvellous. The part of Cranbury Road School which is still standing was the infants'. My first teacher was a lovely lady, Mrs Trent. We had assembly each morning, sitting cross-legged on the wooden floor. One day I put my hands on this as I was standing up and hooked a splinter right the way down my finger to the palm of my hand. A teacher very carefully picked all the splinter out, wiped the wound with TCP, bandaged it then I was sent home with a letter from the headmistress, Miss Michie, explaining what had happened. Later I went on to Mrs Green's class, then Miss Patterson's. It was such a joy going to school. Then I went up to the junior school, where there were still air raid shelters in the playground. I was in Miss Randall's class. We didn't have lockers, just an area with clothes pegs and you pegged up your PE kit and wellies, but no-one ever stole anything. At the end of each academic year you had to line up and be divided into two classes for the next year. One teacher, Miss Darter, was tall and thin, very strict. My name was called out for her class and my world fell apart, I was dreading September. But she taught me to knit, and I've been an avid knitter since. Unfortunately, I have arthritis now. She also taught us the rudiments of gardening as well. Then came Miss Brown's class. I thought she was ancient, say about eighty when she taught us. Her hair was always straight back in a bun and she wore dowdy clothes. Yet years later my mother often saw her at the hairdressers, so she must have been a lot younger than I thought.

In those days the 11+ was in two parts, if you passed the first then you sat part 2. Obviously I was very borderline because I was called for interview at Eastleigh County High School, which I went to after getting through that daunting process. No sooner was I there when they announced they were going to build Barton Peveril Grammar School on one of the corn fields.

In Monks Way, I had a south-facing bedroom with open views and land nearby eventually became allotments. An uncle who was going on two weeks' holiday said to Mum, 'Help yourself to any produce from my patch, it's all ripe, shame to let it rot.' So we did. My uncle returned and said, 'You really should have helped yourself from my allotment.' We told him we had. Whose allotment we picked from we never knew – they must have thought there were thieves about.

I married in 1963 and left Monks Way. We lived in a few places in Southampton, where we worked, then bought this house in Colden Common in 1968. We go into Eastleigh quite a bit. It's not full of mobile phone shops like some towns.

ANN BURNETT
née Mallender, Docking

Campbell Road had a street party for VE Day in 1945, when I was six. I didn't understand what it was about but remember the happy atmosphere and dashing about playing chase with the other children. There were also regular fancy dress competitions and Mum would make outfits for me and my brother Roger, who was sixteen months older. I shared a bed with Roger, which my grandchildren think is very strange, but everyone had double beds in those days where quite a number of children would have to squeeze in together.

I can still remember the names of neighbours in Campbell Road, it was a cosy place. When I was four, my mother taught me to knit which I really

VE celebrations in Campbell Road, 1945. (Ann Burnett)

enjoyed. I started school at Cranbury Road and soon realised I was not at all academic – my confidence sapped a little. When I was about eight I knitted myself a jumper at home, it was emerald green with a black fir tree design all up the front. I was so proud of it and took it into school to show my teacher. She was amazed, told the class how clever I was – 'look at the neatness, the perfect tension in the stitches.' She took me and my jumper round every class in the school and I felt so good about myself, I'll never forget that day.

Also when I was eight, Roger and I were told Mum was expecting a baby. A week later, after we'd gone to bed, there was a lot of commotion, neighbours running up and down the stairs to see Mum who'd said she wasn't feeling too well. The grown-ups kept closing our bedroom door and we kept opening it a little. They kept closing it again. We couldn't sleep and eventually heard a baby crying. A little later I could have sworn the noise came from two babies. We weren't allowed to go into Mum's bedroom until the following morning. Again, I was so proud when I went to school and told my teacher and class-mates that we had two new babies in our house. No. 28 was always full of little friends who wanted to play with the twins.

I went on to Chamberlayne Road School for Girls and loved sport. I was put in for the Hampshire Athletic Trials with another girl called Mary Wing. We didn't get through but were proud to have reached that far. At an Eastleigh Inter-School Sports Day a girl told me that a boy called Ivor Docking, competing for Toynbee Road School, liked me. I didn't take much notice. At a later sports event, someone said Ivor wanted to see me. I said I'd talk to him but didn't want a boyfriend. So we became friends and eventually I agreed to become his girlfriend as long as there was no kissing. We were both aged fourteen and I really believed that if you kissed a boy, you had a baby!

As a schoolgirl I did a morning paper round for Gregory's Newsagents and earned 7s 6d, 5s of which went to Holloways Cycle Shop in Market Street as weekly payments for the bike I'd bought. Mum let me keep the remainder, as pocket money for sweets, etc. I never let on I bought lipstick as I wasn't allowed to wear make up. For face powder, my friends and I used to put flour on our faces. On the way to school, I'd stop in the telephone kiosk further down Campbell Road and take my socks off – I always went to school with bare legs, even in the winter.

At fifteen, I got a job as a stitcher in Caustons. You'd sit at a machine, put an open book on it, press the foot pedal and the book would be stitched together, a bit like staples. Caustons had lots of departments. Some people were folders where they fed the printed sheets into a machine and the pages came out folded the other side. It was a happy place, I loved going to work. There'd be a bonus rate if we achieved our maximum target, so we worked like the clappers yet still had a laugh.

Ivor stayed on at Toynbee to take his O Levels and then did an apprenticeship at Pirelli's to be an electrical engineer. In 1960 we married at the parish church, which was converted into flats some years ago.

We rented our first home in Oaktree Caravan Park down Allington Lane. That caravan was a dear little lovenest. It was only 22ft long and the bed folded up against the wall when you weren't sleeping. We both cycled into work, I'd go 3 miles to the other side of Eastleigh and Ivor to Millbrook, 6 miles, where he'd got a job at Mullards, as it was then. It later became Phillips.

Ivor was keen to emigrate to Australia, so in 1965, when our first son was a baby, we paid our £10 assisted passage and sailed off. Australia was good, we had a beautiful modern spacious house and excellent standard of living, but I was homesick. Back in England, I'd spent every Wednesday in Campbell Road with my mother, who loved cuddling the baby. I always

Parish church as flats, 2011.

missed those midweek chatty days. It was a shock in 1966 to hear Mum had died suddenly. I was devastated but couldn't afford to fly back to Eastleigh for the funeral. By then we'd had another son. Although we made lots of friends, after two years in Adelaide we decided to save for the passage home. Some years later, my sister Rosemarie told me she'd often found our Mum at the bottom of the garden on a Wednesday, shedding a tear because she missed me so much. That still me makes me feel sad.

We came back to Eastleigh and were back to square one. We lived with Ivor's parents in Drake Road, Bishopstoke, for twenty months before getting a council house in Fryern Road, Chandler's Ford. After five years, my eldest brother Alf and his wife Margaret said we were silly paying rent and one night made us sit down with them and go through our budget. It was obvious, if we put our minds to it, that we could save quite easily for a deposit because Ivor had a good job. A year later we bought a brand new house in Petworth Gardens, Boyatt Wood. We watched it being built and lived very happily there until 1983.

Clicked between poses. Ann's wedding day at the parish church. Mum Martha is far left, while Tony is behind the small bridesmaid (niece Frances). Rosemarie is the bridesmaid to the left behind Tony. The other bridesmaid is niece Valerie. (Ann Burnett)

Ann and Ivor Docking with sons Shaun and Grant, plus sister-in-law Margaret at the back, visit 6 Petworth Gardens as it was being built. (Ann Burnett)

But then my world shattered – Ivor died suddenly of a heart attack. He was only forty-four and I was completely lost without him. A year later Shaun, my eldest son, was offered a sports scholarship in America and Grant left school at sixteen and moved away to work. Suddenly I was all on my own. It was horrible and I was in a right state. However, 'baby' brother Tony was a brick and he'd ring to see how I was and take me out every Sunday. We'd often walk along the River Itchen at Bishopstoke, that was very soothing.

The happy memories in 6 Petworth Gardens seemed to echo around the house, which I found upsetting, so I bought a bungalow in Whalesmead Road, Bishopstoke. I worked at Paul's Fish and Chip Shop, which took me out seeing people. Eventually my sister-in-law persuaded me to have a blind date with a man called Sid Burnett. In 1989 I married Sid and had many happy years together.

We moved to this new ground floor flat in Chandler's Ford just before Sid became seriously ill. I lost him at the end of 2008.

Nowadays I go to Fleming Park for swimming, keep fit and I cycle regularly. I often go into Eastleigh, buy my wool at the market. Shaun is forty-seven and soon to be a father for the first time, so I'm busy knitting for my third grandchild, looking forward to another trip to South Carolina. Then I must get to grips with Skype!

ROSEMARIE HEMMING
née Mallender, Burgess

Rosemarie is the sister of Ann Burnett.

My Dad, Fred Mallender, came from Yorkshire. He was in the Army which brought him down south where he met my mum, Martha Buxey. Mum was born and bred in Titchfield and married Dad when he got a job at the railway works in Campbell Road. They were living in rooms in Eastleigh with their first baby, Amy, before they were allocated a council house in Derby Road in about 1930. A second child, Alfred, was born there. In 1932, Dad was offered a railway house in Campbell Road which was very convenient and also cheaper – 2s a week was a lot of money in those days! Five years later my brother Roger was born at no. 28 followed by sister Ann in 1939.

In July 1947 my mother felt unwell, and asked Nurse Jefferies, the local nurse, to examine her. She said, 'Congratulations, Mrs Mallender, you're five months pregnant. And you've two babies kicking around in there!'

This was quite a shock for my mother who was forty-one – her eldest daughter was already married with a toddler. Twenty-one-year-old Amy was disgusted by what Mum and Dad had been up to. At their age! She even refused to speak to our Dad for a while.

He was enjoying a pint at the British Legion when Mum went into labour. Amy was sent to bring him home but he said, 'Oh, she won't have them yet awhile.'

Nurse Jefferies sent her back again to get him.

'It's a boy,' She told Dad. 'You gotta get home quick.'

'Oh,' said Dad. 'A boy! This calls for another pint.' Yet again, Amy was furious with him. So I was the youngest, born 25 minutes after Tony.

Tony and Rosemarie, summer 1948. (Ann Burnett)

Children didn't have a room to themselves in those days. I shared a double bed with Ann until she married, I was thirteen then. It felt strange sleeping on my own. Until Tony was ten, he was in with Roger. We used to have pillow fights, although once a pillow burst and feathers flew everywhere – Dad went ballistic.

As a family we listened to the radio, especially *The Archers*. Bedtime was always 7 o'clock and Dad would peel us an apple before we went to bed. We would watch fascinated, waiting to see which one of us had the longest peel.

I think the Alexander family opposite us were the first to have a TV. That was an amazing novelty; all the kids would crowd into their house to watch *Children's Hour*.

Our house in Campbell Road had three bedrooms, two rooms downstairs plus the kitchen. The toilet was outside, though attached to the house (we didn't have to walk to the bottom of the garden – quite a luxury). There was no bathroom but Mum considered us lucky as we had a bath in the kitchen, and not just a tin one hanging on a hook. The bath was big and Victorian-style;

it had a roll top on which was placed a large block of wood. Mum covered this with a colourful oilcloth.

We had no hot water before the late 1950s, just the copper boiler. Mum heated this up on Sundays, our weekly bath night. She'd fill the bath by emptying the boiler with a bucket and because I was the youngest I was the first in, then everyone else took turns. No. 28 was a mid-terrace. We had one source of heating – a coal fire. One of our chores was to go out collecting wood for the fire.

Sunday was roast dinner day and to make good use of the oven Mum baked lots of cakes and puddings. Life was hard for her. She always walked into Eastleigh, almost a mile away, and loads of shopping was needed for a large family. There were no fridges or freezers, no vacuum cleaner – we had lino on the floor and some rugs which Mum hung over the washing line for beating. She'd get my brothers to do that.

Rosemarie and friend from next door Christina Peart, both aged seven. (Rosemarie Hemming)

We had a curtain hung on a wire above the bath. During the week Mum put the dirty washing into it, took it all out on Sunday so we could have our bath then she'd put the soiled clothes back to soak in the used bathwater, ready for Monday's wash day. There was a mangle outside where she'd wring the clean washing to put on the line. She always had jobs do.

Dad worked in the machine shop down the bottom of the road where he eventually became a chargehand. Back in the Second World War he was also in the Railway Fire Brigade. Everyone around us worked in the railway. Once a year there'd be an open day, and employees' families could get in free. We had rail passes, so we enjoyed lots of train journeys. As children we grew up using the trains, not cars like they do these days. Cars were expensive.

During the working week, the Eastleigh end of Campbell Road was a sight to remember at 12 noon and 5 o'clock. The men had an hour's lunch break and would stream out, cycling to their homes for a hot dinner. Then home time was prompt at 5 and the road was a sea of men. Buses never ventured near Campbell Road at those times. Trainspotters were always around but I don't think we noticed the steam trains chugging past, we'd been used to them since we were tiny.

Dad enjoyed his work but unfortunately he developed emphysema (he was a heavy smoker, like so many people in those days). Eventually he became too ill to work, though we still could live in our railway cottage.

Campbell Road was a place of its own, isolated from Eastleigh. Railway lines were near the backs of both rows of houses and no-one had a reason to come into it unless they lived there or worked at the railway. It was nicknamed Spike Island because it was surrounded by spiked railings.

At the bottom of the road we had a playing field which backed onto what was Eastleigh airport but not many planes flew over in those days. Campbell Road houses had allotments, so everyone grew their own vegetables. We had to help with the weeding, the boys digging up potatoes and veg.

Down the bottom of the road was a pig farm ran by Mr Groves. He came around collecting food scraps to feed his pigs, and he also kept chickens. Eggs weren't called free-range then – all eggs were from hens who enjoyed fresh air.

Everyone looked after each other. Mothers in Campbell Road rarely walked small children to school because there were responsible older ones to take them. We'd march off together to the Crescent School, and the same again for Saturday morning pictures at the Regal.

On 5 November there'd be a bonfire down at the field. It was built from everyone's broken furniture and rubbish, no-one ever set fire to it before Bonfire Night, when some mums would organise jacket potatoes. Such fun. We had sparklers, no fireworks. In summertime there'd be big picnics, and we loved to do 'roly polys' down the hill and play rounders or cricket. We were never bored. Friends from town came over to share our freedom and you felt safe – there was never any trouble.

We played out all the time, not just at the fields. Alleyways between the houses were great for playing hide and seek (or kiss chase). We could get over the railway line because they weren't electric then and we'd play along the river. Boys made dens or fished while we girls liked to play make-believe. We'd go off on our own for the whole day, taking sandwiches and bottle of water – yes, it was really idyllic.

A loud hooter boomed out at 4.55. This meant the railway workers could leave in five minutes. We children had to be home before the hooter went off. We'd race home, 'Ah, help! Gotta get back! Quick! Quick!' If we were still out and the hooter sounded, we knew we were in trouble. Tea was always on the table at 5 p.m. and naughty late children would either have to eat it cold or make do with leftovers. The others, already at table, were quick to polish off cakes and puddings.

We had to go the parish church for Sunday School and collect our attendance stamps. Then we progressed to the youth club in the parish hall where Sainsbury's car park is now. All the kids went there. I really enjoyed the club, always lots of activities. My brothers went to the Boys' Club which was just over the hill towards Bishopstoke. There was an outside swimming pool next door – brrr, it was always freezing but we swam a lot in the summer. The pool was a popular meeting place and children organised their own social lives. We weren't driven to the formal activities children have now, my parents certainly would not have had the money. We always walked into Eastleigh and the last bus home was 10'o clock (there was only one bus an hour). It had to be the 9 o'clock bus until I was sixteen, then I was allowed an extra hour out. There'd be major trouble if I was late home.

Campbell Road celebrates the royal wedding of Prince Charles and Lady Diana Spencer in July 1981. (Rosemarie Hemming)

My earliest memory is sitting in our twin pram (babies sat in those huge prams until aged two or three). My brother and I were given an ice cream, I was enjoying mine until he finished his and grabbed my cornet. I remember crying – that's brothers for you!

The pram was demolished when Tony and I were about four. I remember we stood at the kitchen window watching our Dad chop it up. The body was made of wood, the exterior was metal and Dad made a cart for our older brothers to play on. Any wood leftover was made into sticks for the fire.

My first day at school (the Crescent C of E) is a vivid memory. I was very nervous and not allowed to sit at the same table as Tony. After school dinner, Tony was sick so he was being taken home. They asked if I wanted to go with him but by then I was engrossed with my crayons, so said no. As soon as he had gone, I started to cry but had to stay till the end of school. I was really frightened because he wasn't with me.

At eleven years old, I moved up to Chamberlayne Road School for Girls and Tony went to Toynbee. By this time, our Dad was very weak with emphysema. He had a bed in the downstairs front room with an oxygen cylinder by the headboard. Sadly he died when we were thirteen. That must have been very difficult for our Mum.

I left school at fifteen and my sister got me a job at Caustons the printers because she was already there. It was either Pirelli, the railway or Caustons for factory work.

One day when I was eighteen, I went to wake Mum up – it was unusual for her to oversleep. She wouldn't budge and we ran to a neighbour who was in the St John Ambulance. She'd had a sudden heart attack, so we sadly lost her as well. By that time, I was married but living at home. We took the council tenancy over, decorated throughout the house and tried to modernise it a bit. Like a lot of people in Campbell Road, we built a lean-to outside the kitchen so we could go to the loo without getting wet in the rain! We still had the bath in the kitchen but by then Formica was available so we covered the old wooden top with that. Instead of a copper boiler, I filled the bath with hot water from a twin-tub washing machine. My three children began life thinking baths belonged in kitchens! A proper bathroom was eventually put in one of the bedrooms, making it a two-bedroom house when Swaythling Housing Association took over the houses in the mid-1970s.

My children too played down the field, although the railway line became electric and fenced off, so they couldn't get to the river like we did. They enjoyed a lot of freedom, more so than living in the town.

I continued to live in Campbell Road until I was thirty-seven. I'd never known anything except the street where I was born so had mixed feelings about leaving. By then the airport had become busier with more planes coming over and the houses were sold off – the majority of residents weren't railway people anymore and no-one knew their neighbours. Buying a modern house in Boyatt Wood with a new husband was exciting.

I still have friends in Campbell Road and often visit. It feels weird that I spent most of my life there. So much has changed – in our childhood hardly any cars drove along, whereas now you need parking permits to visit someone there. But I think growing up in such a friendly community gave me a good start in life.

JAN MAGDZIARZ

After the Second World War there were several camps in the Eastleigh area for Polish people – two in Chestnut Avenue, one where the Warner-Hudnut factory was later built and the other where Asda hypermarket is now. There was one at Hiltingbury and another near Velmore Farm. There was also a camp for English people.

My parents arrived at a dependants camp in Stockbridge on 2 November 1946. I still have all their documents. They'd experienced a difficult journey from Austria, where they'd spent the war years in a German labour camp, through to Torni Camp, Italy. They made their way to France by train and came over to Dover from Calais.

In 1947 they moved to the Hiltingbury camp where I was born a year later, then in 1949 to the Chestnut Avenue site where Asda now is. Our address was Hut 12, Camp 27 and there we stayed until 1956. We had communal outside toilets, Elsan pans which were emptied once a week. You can imagine how they smelled, like portaloos at the end of a rock festival. Yes, those were the bucket and chuck it days! Most families in the camps purchased their own tin baths or you could have a weekly soak in the communal bath-house. For heating we had circular stoves with a flue going through the roof, fed on coke or coal. It would be red hot but children knew they were dangerous so didn't go near them. They knew burns were painful, so kept well away.

For a child, life in camp was absolutely wonderful. We used to run and run through the woods and fields, play all day, sneak into orchards and go scrumping, lots of fun and laughter. We'd go all the way to Fleming Park which was nothing like it is now, just playing fields and a wooden pavilion with changing rooms.

Language was not a problem for the children. I can't remember the transition of speaking Polish all the time at home, and then switching automatically to English at school or in the Eastleigh shops. Schooling was

Nissen huts at Velmore Camp. (Len Harvell)

at the Holy Cross School, behind the Catholic church. The pupils were aged from four to fifteen. How they packed so many children into the building I don't know – it looks so small if you look at it now! The Polish children also had to attend Saturday morning school to keep up our native language. That was tedious sometimes because it meant you missed Saturday morning pictures at the Regal – I did bunk off sometimes!

In 1956 we moved to Hamilton Road, Bishopstoke. When people left the camps to live in allotted council houses, we seemed to get separated. The majority did move to Bishopstoke, but others went to Netley, Hamble or different parts of Southampton.

I went to Bishopstoke Infants School in Church Lane and then Stoke Park Junior. Childhood in Bishopstoke continued to be an adventure; we had Stoke Park Woods on one side and then the River Itchen and fields on the other. That attraction of Bishopstoke still remains, people love living there because of the woods and the river.

I cycled from Bishopstoke to Hamble to play football, that's quite a hike by bike. It was fine going there but difficult if you injured yourself during the game as you still had to cycle home; there were no mobile phones then! Ordinary people didn't have landlines or even cars.

One happy memory is the Boys' Club at Bishopstoke. They had so many activities, all kinds of sports, weight-lifting, gymnastics, boxing, etc. Why they stopped Boys' Clubs, I'll never know. It's not politically correct and might sound sexist, but it was just what young boys needed. You had to behave, no stepping out of line, no bullying allowed; it had a self-regulating structure. There were fabulous chaps involved with it: Bill Bailey, Sandy Powell and Skipper Granger, all very inspirational. I discovered a talent for boxing and eventually went from amateur to professional. I still go boxing training now.

Near to the Boys' Club was the open-air swimming pool which everyone loved. It seems to me that if people like something too much, it's got rid of. Also, we could swim down the river to the barge. If you came down from The Mount, through the woods, you came to the bend and there's quite deep water there. It was a lovely area, you could swim, have picnics. I remember, in the early 1960s, salmon coming up the river. There's a bridge by what is now the

First pages of the Aliens' Registration Certificate belonging to Jan Magdziarz's father. (Jan Magdziarz)

River Inn Toby Carvery (which was Dr Boyle's house and surgery). You could just stand there and watch these huge salmon making their way upriver. We lads enjoyed fishing too.

In 1966 a youth club in Nightingale Avenue was opened by Princess Margaret. It's gone now – been knocked down – but I had my picture taken with the queen's sister.

For secondary education I went to the Wyvern School in Desborough Road. There is now a Wyvern School in Fair Oak but the old Wyvern was in a large Victorian building which is still there. We went to Eastleigh Technical College for metalwork and technical drawing. While still at school, I had a morning paper round in Eastleigh, an evening paper round plus a Saturday job at Fine Fare supermarket. That was then what they would today call my EMA (Education Maintenance Allowance). If we wanted money, we had to earn it.

I went on to do a five-year apprenticeship in Winchester. I've enjoyed my working life in engineering though there was a time when on top of full-time hours I was boxing professionally too. That became particularly stressful and tiring. More recently, I was made redundant after twenty-five years, tried running my own business which was fine until the recession hit. So I'm now retired – but with no time on my hands.

I left Eastleigh in 1973 when I married. My parents continued to live there and my father had no urge to return to Poland. One of his friends went back and we never heard anything from him. We often wonder what happened to him. Dad thought England was absolutely wonderful. He would never ever say a word against the UK. As far as he was concerned, it was the best thing that could have happened to him. Strange how life turned out for them: from Poland, Austria, Italy, to Stockbridge, eventually Bishopstoke. If we hadn't moved to Hamilton Road I'd have never been to the Boys' Club and discovered boxing.

JAN GACA

I lived in Eastleigh for sixty years though I was born in Italy. Shortly after the Second World War broke out, the Germans conscripted Polish people and sent them to labour camps in Austria; my parents were among these. When the war finished, they made their way to join the allies in southern Italy, and came to England by boat in September 1946. We were sent straight to Hiltingbury camp near Chandler's Ford – I was one year old. After two years, once my father had served his time in the army over in Italy, we moved to the camp in Chestnut Avenue where the Warner-Hudnut site used to be.

For children, camp life was brilliant. Besides all the daytime out playing, on Saturday night people would congregate in Jan M's hut as his parents were musicians. The beds in the huts were separated from the living area by a curtain, so the children would be put to bed for the night, curtain drawn across while the adults sang and danced until the early hours.

Life must have been difficult for our parents; transport was not as it is now and we couldn't afford what there was. My Dad worked on a building site, that's why they were over, the UK needed labour to help rebuild it. Then he worked for Esso at the Fawley Refinery, where they were bussed from the camps down to the other end of Southampton Water. He'd come home with his wage packet: £2 18s 11d and out of that he paid rent, which was £1 17s 8d. That didn't leave much for heating, food, clothes, etc. for four children. My mother kept chickens and rabbits to support the family. The hens roamed all over the place and we used to play 'hunt the eggs' in the woods. At the time we didn't realise what fun it was, but when you look back and compare what today's children have, it was paradise. So safe and free. I remember going to the Bottle and Jug, an off licence part of a public house, to buy beer for my Dad when I was only nine. We were also sent to buy cigarettes.

The Gaca children in 1953. Left to right: sister Theresa, next a cousin, in pram youngest sister Grazyna, then Jan aged 8 and then brother Zygmund. (Jan Gaca)

In 1956 we moved to a house in Hamilton Road, Bishopstoke, which my parents were thrilled with. Having no contact with their family back in Poland must have been upsetting and I did feel sorry for them. When they were young and forced into labour camps, they never saw their families again. My father sent money to his people. He'd put a 10s note along with a letter in an envelope but his gift never reached them. Eventually he learned the trick of encasing the money in a sheet of carbon paper. That always got there safely. Much later, my father's mother did come to stay with us in Bishopstoke. What a worker she was, she'd be digging the garden at 5 in the morning. She'd dug half of it by the time I woke up.

My biggest memory is when the men all came out of the carriage works for lunch. At noon they would emerge to cycle home, then back again for the hooter at five to one. Such a swarm of men, Bishopstoke Bridge would be crammed with bikes. Unbelievable. That fascinating sight will always stick with me. Billy Cotton would come to their canteen to record *Workers' Playtime* which I heard on the radio. It was sad when the carriage works closed. Also Pirelli, Caustons and Prices. There are some people who wanted to live on the Park 21 estate because they worked all their lives in Pirelli.

Those big companies looked after their workers in the sense that they had a sports club, playing fields, tennis courts, social club, outings, etc. I got a job at Pirelli when I was saving to get married. The money was good but I can't say I liked the work at first, very monotonous but at least close to home. The jointers at that time were getting 6s 4d an hour. Pirelli had many contracts abroad and the one in India paid the labourers a halfpenny an hour in old sterling.

Our family moved to Twyford Road. Then, when I married, I lived in The Crescent before moving a few times, staying in Eastleigh until four years ago when we came to Rownhams. Jan and I see a lot of each other, especially as my youngest daughter married his son and we now share a granddaughter.

Once it became easy to get into Poland I visited the country and was surprised how, when I crossed the border, tears came to my eyes. Since then, we've bought a flat in the mountains there, so I think our ancestors would be proud that we've survived and made successes of our lives.

Daughter of Jan G., left, marries son of Jan M., right in 2008. (Jan Gaca)

MIKE WINTER

I was christened immediately after being born in Winchester hospital as they thought I wasn't going to live. That was in 1946. At that time my parents were renting one room in Desborough Road; with a baby and my four-year-old elder brother it must have been a squash.

After the war, when Dad left the army, my mother's father got him a job in the railway. Life was like that then, if a member of your family worked for the railway, then you too could have a job there. It was the same in all the big companies in Eastleigh.

I was still small when the family moved to a brand new council house. What luxury! There was a bathroom upstairs plus a toilet downstairs – two loos! Downstairs 'cloakrooms' were not the norm then. I believe we were the first family to move into Starling Square. The council provided a range in the living room for heating plus a gas cooker in the kitchen. There was a big square sink which still remained when I got married. All the estate roads were named after birds: Raven Square, Dove Dale, Jackdaw Rise and so on. Everyone called it the 'Bird Aviary'. Heinz Burt the pop star grew up in the Aviary – indeed, I went to school with his brother.

As children we'd play all over the place. I mixed with Polish and Italian refugees at school, so we'd cycle up to Velmore Camp to see them. We ran around and cycled safely all around the Bird Aviary as there were only about four cars on the whole estate until I was about ten years old. They'd be called 'wrecks' today, the MOT didn't exist then – they'd never get through it! Nearly everyone grew their own vegetables and kept chickens or rabbits. We had chickens. A chicken was a special treat, like for Christmas dinner; I was eleven before we ate turkey.

My first school was in Stoneham Lane, where the Concorde Club is now, and my secondary modern was North End. The boys and girls had classes together but the playgrounds were separate.

Inside one of the Pirelli industrial sheds prior to demolition, November 2001. (Eastleigh Borough Council)

Jobs were plentiful when I left school at Easter aged fifteen – I was working three days later. I'd two offers already but Dad worked at Pirelli by then and arranged an interview for me. The first thing they asked was 'Have you any family working here?' There were no apprenticeships going, so I started off as an Odd Job Boy in the Joint Room, sweeping the floor, running errands, soldering sockets. I was always sent to get the pies. At 9 a.m. the canteen opened and you could buy these huge meat pies. I've never tasted or smelled anything like them since, my mouth waters at the thought of them. If faggots were on the menu, they were the size of cannonballs. They provided one of the best workers' canteens and even if you were retired from the firm, you could go to the canteen and get meals at staff prices.

My first wages were £3 7s 6d. When I was eighteen I started shift work. I can still picture those cable reels. Huge, weighed 50 ton, they were unbelievable. I also became an Industrial Fireman as the company had its own fire brigade. Pirelli became the biggest employer in Eastleigh – 2,000 people I believe when I worked there. Every Christmas you were allowed to buy two pairs of quality Pirelli slippers at a huge discount from the company shop on the site. I think everyone in Eastleigh wore similar slippers!

Pirelli being demolished, February 2002. (Eastleigh Borough Council)

The social club was one of the best in the country. Young lads could play snooker if accompanied by an adult. I loved table tennis, too. The Pirelli club had all sports facilities, including a swimming pool. It even had its own library.

I always remember the brilliant Eastleigh Carnival where each department of the railway, e.g. the paint shop, wagon works, carriage works, engine shed, etc. would try to outdo each other with floats. These were always spectacular.

All the big employers in Eastleigh put on superb parties for the children. People would put a couple of bob in per week and their kids went to the Christmas party. Firms spent an absolute fortune on presents for kids. Some got train sets and pushbikes and with so many local relatives, many children went to two parties. I did and so did my children.

My Mum worked at Prices Bakery. When we were small she worked in the evening, picking me up from school on the bike, and off we'd go to the bakery. She'd take me into the ladies' changing rooms (at five years old it didn't matter). Then she'd put me behind the boxes where they stored the cakes. Mum worked on the slab cakes, when she wasn't looking I used to pick the nuts off the top of them. Later she did full-time hours, which meant we could go away on holiday every year. I spent that time of my life coming home to a dinner placed in the fridge, covered in tin foil, which I had to heat up by placing it on a saucepan of boiling water for about 20 minutes. No microwaves then, yuck, those dinners were awful. I threw away more meals than I ate.

As working teenagers we started going to dances. Top Rank in Southampton insisted you wore a tie and decent footwear – no jeans, no trainers (well, in those days we had plimsolls).

By 1973 I was a married man with a mortgage and one child. What amused me back then is that I was more than happy to push the pram down the High Street while other men would take the mickey.

'Not a man's job,' they'd say. I didn't care. I used to push my little sister down to Fleming Park when I was fourteen and I enjoyed it even if the other lads thought me strange. Better to get us both out of the house, where there was only the radio. If you had a telly, it didn't start until four in the afternoon.

When I go into Eastleigh now it's strange to see all the changes. I've no relatives there, all my mother's family became Ten Pound Poms. It's sad to remember that Pirelli has all gone. Like everyone else, I was made redundant in 2002. I'm still doing shift work, seven days on/four days off as a porter at Southampton General Hospital. Makes you appreciate good health.

SUE WINTER

I met Mike at Pirelli in the Telephone Cabling Department where we both worked. It's amazing how many couples got together in those big Eastleigh companies. I went over to the factory at Bishopstoke when that opened, in about 1969.

There were twenty-six in my class when I left school in 1963 aged fifteen. We all started work on the Monday following end of term. There were no careers advisors then.

I first went to Edwin Jones department store (Debenhams) and earned £1 10s a week. Then someone said her sister earned good money at Pirelli. Off I went and earned £9, though we worked shifts to earn it. To me, going to work on a sunny summer's afternoon is deathly. Other people are getting towards the end of their working day and it'll be dark when you get home with everyone going to bed.

I started by making telephone cables and after three years moved to the Testing Department which I liked. It was day shift only, more money and you didn't get your hands dirty.

In 1971, a few years after we married we'd saved a deposit for a house. We bought our first home in Doncaster Road for £2,990. The road had terraced houses which were built for railway workers and at the other end semi-detached houses built for managers. The price difference when we were house hunting was £500, which we couldn't afford. Our terraced house, no. 24, was comfortable, very spacious and we lived there for ten years.

We had two daughters while living in Doncaster Road. I must say that, to me, the town wasn't very friendly if they didn't know you. Where I'd been brought up in St Denys everyone said hullo and smiled, even if they were strangers. People looked at me a bit weird when I did this pushing the pram down the High Street, so I stopped.

Later I worked at the old Railway Institute, where Sainsbury's is now. It fitted in with the children as we could take them in with us during school holidays while we did our cleaning. The boss was very good to working mums; the children could kick a ball about in the function room or play snooker – if it wasn't for that, I couldn't have worked. It's funny looking back, so many of those clubs in Eastleigh were men-only – women certainly weren't allowed to play snooker. The Railway Institute moved over to its new site in Romsey Road while I was working there but I much preferred the homely old building.

One memory is of sitting in Doncaster Road at 10 p.m. one night when Mike was at work. There was this awful roar, a dreadful loud blast; I thought the end of the world had come. What I'd heard was the first jet plane taking off from the airport, which we lived fairly close to. Until then all the planes had propellers and it certainly made me jump out of my skin. One thing that does annoy us is that it's called Southampton Airport but it's in Eastleigh. I bet a lot of people were disgruntled when the name was changed.

MALCOLM CLARKE

talks about Eastleigh Football Club

My family moved to Chandler's Ford when I was four. Eventually I moved away but in 1988 I returned to the area, watching an Eastleigh FC match within the first week, and probably wanted to get involved from day one. In the second season I helped with the programme. The following season I became Joint Programme Editor, then took on the role of Press Officer.

Our football club was formed in 1946 by Derik Brooks and today he is Life President at the age of eighty-seven. The team was formerly known as Swaythling Athletic and changed its name to Eastleigh in about 1980. They played at a ground in Walnut Avenue but moved to the present site in Stoneham Lane in 1957.

Our highlights have included winning the Wessex League in 2002/03. We then achieved three promotions in successive years which got us into

Eastleigh Football Club's first team, August 2011. (Mike Denning)

the Blue Square Bet Conference South, two divisions below the lowest level of the Football League. We are doing well in that and also got to the FA Cup first round proper. Pretty good for a small town like Eastleigh. Having Matt le Tissier playing for us has been a bonus. Paul Doswell, formerly a player, came as manager and gave a lot of money to the club. He has now left, and other local businessmen such as Paul Murray (Chairman) financially support the club.

Obviously a lot has changed in the twenty-three years I've been going. We have good facilities now and it's such a friendly club, I love going there. The social club is thriving and it's good to meet people.

We have a scheme where youngsters can get in free or at reduced rates and there are lots of teams for younger players. Sometimes they can be mascots and it means a lot to a youngster to be a mascot. We like to encourage enthusiasm. We are also now introducing a scheme which will bring in younger players because our average age has been quite high. It's a question of getting the right balance between experience and youth, quite a novel experiment. We're looking forward to the future, it'll be interesting to see how our new scheme works.

BOB FIELDSEND

The houses around here were built in 1898, so on 27 June 1998 we held a centenary street party. It took six months to organise and about twelve of us teamed up. We managed to get donations for everything we needed with Les Smith the butcher providing sausages and burgers, and other businesses giving soft drinks, beer, party decorations, etc.

A big barbecue was built by a company up the road who also donated charcoals. We had an articulated truck at the end of our no-through street (Barton Road) which became the base for a covered stage. Performing on this we had a Chas & Dave tribute duo, a DJ and a neighbour's band played

live music too. Lynn and I go line dancing, so we had a session teaching people to do that. We dressed as a pearly king and queen and most people entered the spirit of the occasion by dressing in the style of 1898.

Pearly king and queen – Bob and Lynn Fieldsend, June 1998. (Bob Fieldsend)

Centenary celebrations in Barton Road, Bishopstoke, June 1998. (Southern Daily Echo)

My son Martin served ice cream from one of those pushbikes with a huge ice box at the front and we had two long lines of tables down the street which became packed with residents of all ages from the close vicinity. What fun we had! What was so strange that day is the rest of Eastleigh had rain, torrential rain sometimes, but just over our little area it stayed dry and sunny. That will always stay with me.

We started setting up in the morning and then the mayor officially opened the party. She looked like Hyacinth Bucket from the TV comedy *Keeping Up Appearances*, which we thought added to the atmosphere. Then we partied until 2 in the morning!

* * *

We bought the newsagents at 14 Bishopstoke Road in 1987. For twenty years I'd worked at A.C. Delco and was desperate to get off the factory floor and do my own thing. We settled for a life of long hours and hard work but never regretted it; I still get up at 5 a.m. and we don't close until 6 in the evening. It's a great job if you like talking to people and being your own boss. We've always been an open house.

Back when we opened we mainly sold newspapers, magazines, sweets and cigarettes. However, the newspaper trade has dwindled drastically, so we don't stock a large amount. Also, there is a petrol station opposite now which sells papers, as do all the supermarkets, plus people read news online. We used to employ paperboys but they were often unreliable and I'd have to do deliveries myself. I don't think today's youngsters like getting up early or going out in pouring rain and cold winds.

Our main trade now is home made rolls. We make everything fresh in the morning, wrap them individually in cling film and they're very popular with people who work nearby. We get to know customers' favourites and pander to special requests.

Another change I've noticed is that people don't talk so much; they seem in such a rush these days. The older folk still like to linger and have a chat, a lot of them we've known for twenty-odd years now – the things some people tell you! One ol' boy always asks for things to cure ailments in his nether regions.

An unusual sight outside would happen every day the first few years we were here as the farmer from down the other end of Dutton Lane would herd his cattle up that lane and across the main road to another field. All the traffic had to stop while the cows mooed and shuffled to the other side, quite unbelievable!

Back in the days of the centenary street party I knew everyone in this road, now I don't know even half of them. So many houses have been turned into flats or bedsits, people come and go quickly. There hasn't been a street party since then and no-one is talking about the Queen's Diamond Jubilee next year. Our last neighbourhood bash was for the Millennium New Year's Eve. Every New Year until 2000, the old Bishopstoke Social Club across the road would let all the locals in and bring an American supper. Then the club closed down and a new one was built some distance away. The Boys' Club used to be nearby too, but of course that doesn't exist any more.

Lots of industrial businesses have closed because of the recession and places like Barton Road are now permit parking only, which we have to pay for – it seems like the world is full of red tape! There's always been a large advertising board on the wall at the side of the shop, where I let local businesses put posters up. It became tatty with age so I replaced it, only to get a letter saying if we didn't take it down there'd be a fine of £1,200. I never charged for the advertising – I was trying to help the local community; that's been a bit of a saga. However, we keep smiling, life's too short.

We'll be selling up in the near future – we want to retire and enjoy ourselves before we're too old. Lynn and I are studying for 'skipper' exams so that we can sail on the waterways. There's about 4,500 miles of waterways in this country. Someone told us it took them a year to do them all and we fancy trying that. The only downside is missing the grandchildren, but imagine chugging along with all that peaceful scenery! I expect we'll still get up early and enjoy the dawn chorus.

RITA MARTIN
née Styles

My father, Bill Styles, worked for all the big companies around here: Pirelli, Caustons and the railway. Both my parents were brought up in the High Street and were living with my Dad's mother at the time I was born. That was at Rookwood Maternity Hospital which no longer exists, but the site has been called Rookwood Close. When I was a few months old, they moved to a council house in Robin Square.

When I look back on my childhood I had a wonderful life. I loved it, we'd play tin can alley in the streets, hopscotch and marbles. I can remember standing on the corner of Nightingale Avenue and Chestnut Avenue, taking car number plates. We'd have a little book, five minutes would go by, no cars, and when one did drive past, we'd often say 'Oh, no, we've got that one!' There were so few cars back then.

A fish and chip van came round the estate as well as a baker, the Corona man and a vegetable chap. My mother didn't need to go to the shops, they all came to her. When it came to recycling, there was the rag and bone man while dustmen would come into the back garden and take your rubbish bin out, carrying it on their backs and emptying it into the lorry.

On Guy Fawkes Night people in our local roads built a communal bonfire which would be where the motorway is now, behind Robin Square. I remember going to the social club of Prices Bakery, previously a village school where my grandma went (it's now the Concorde Club). We'd walk to Stoneham lakes, playing for hours making dens then up to Hut Hill where there was a derelict house. Once a tramp stood in the doorway and shouted at us. We ran like mad, luckily not falling down the open well in the grounds. I shudder when I think of that!

Schooling was at Nightingale Avenue then North End Secondary Modern, which is now the fire station. The school in Chandler's Ford, Thornden, is an anagram of North End.

We loved the old swimming pool at Bishopstoke and I also used the Pirelli pool because Dad worked there. We were never short of places to go, Eastleigh was a nice little town to be brought up in – lots of friends, everyone knew everyone.

There was Clemoes the dress shop. They had two branches, one on the corner of High Street and Leigh Road and one near Woolworths, which of course is gone now. Mum bought broken biscuits from Woolies. I was fascinated by Speeds the wool shop. A little V-shaped shop in Market Street, it was so tiny you couldn't get more than two customers in at a time. It was jam-packed with wool because everyone used to knit in those days. Mum always had knitting on the go.

Teenage years were great fun. I'd go to the Green Hut in Stoneham Lane where Mrs Lomas ran a youth club for thirteen to sixteen year olds; it was

Clemoes the dress shop. (Hampshire Museums and Archives)

Leigh Road, with Woolworths, 1980s. (Len Harvell)

brilliant. She was an amazing youth leader and we did pewter work and country dancing, with mechanics for the boys. She'd invite us to her house in Woodside Avenue and show us how to make potato wine and every year we put together a float for the carnival – Eastleigh did a great carnival back in those days. Then a youth centre in Nightingale Avenue was opened by Princess Margaret, so that was a big thing for us all.

On Sunday afternoons we'd go down to the old Fleming Park; there was a café in the pavilion and we'd hang around there. Every Sunday night a whole crowd of my friends went to the Regal cinema. Opposite, above Burtons, was the Imperial which held discos for youngsters (they didn't serve alcohol). In my teens, of course, was the Mods and Rockers era and all the rockers would go to the Station Café and Junction Hotel while the Mods would go to the Mini Diner in the day and the Chuck Wagon at night. We'd sit in there making a cup of coffee last a long time, with all the scooters parked outside and the lads wearing their hooded parkas. Everyone wore Hush Puppies and thought they looked wonderful. I don't remember any of us drinking alcohol much.

I remember when rumour went around that Billy Fury was at Heinz Burt's parents' house in Sparrow Square. Lots of us girls sat outside, really excited,

Regal cinema, Market Street, 1970s. (Len Harvell)

Heinz Burt (centre, back row) visits home in Sparrow Square with friends including Karl Denver, Marty Wilde and Billy Fury. (David St John)

waiting for him to come out. When he did we were all of a flutter but just smiled and didn't ask for autographs.

Working life began as an office junior for Eastleigh Borough Council in the old town hall. I was promoted to the Land Charges Section, then made secretary to the Deputy Town Clerk. There was a manual typewriter and stencils with that dreadful pink stuff to paint over mistakes. I could type pages and pages of reports; you daren't make mistakes because you'd have to rub them out, especially on all those carbon copies. Tippex fluid seemed a miracle! Then golf ball electric machines with erasing tape came in. Nowadays my typing on the computer is really slapdash, it's all so easy to put right.

After reorganisation took place I worked for the Borough Secretary, then became the mayor's secretary. When I left to have children in 1985, I'd been the chief executive's secretary for three years. At twenty-one, I'd moved from home to live in Totton but returned to Eastleigh when the motorway links became so good. My husband ran his own business and travelled a lot so Boyatt Wood was very convenient. Sadly, he died so I went back to work at the council. Most of my working life has been with them. I'm still never short of things to do, places to go.

VALERIE PEARCE

talks about her job at Fleming Park Leisure Centre

When I turned fifty, a complete change from working full-time in retail management appealed to me. I saw a receptionist vacancy here but not part-time. However, it sounded so interesting I took it and eventually reduced my hours. Now I work four mornings a week plus extra when they are short-staffed.

Fleming Park Leisure Centre opened in October 1974 and some staff have been here since then. One lady on reception is seventy (I'm sixty-two). We all stay because we enjoy our jobs and there's a nice family atmosphere in front of and behind our desk.

About four years ago the centre was refurbished. One reason was the law on disabled access that says everyone should be able to use the same entrance. There were a huge amount of steps at the front before, but now it's lovely and flat with automatic doors. The swimming pool is straight along the corridor on ground level and there are lifts if people want to use the café and other first-floor facilities. There is something here for everybody and for all ages.

There's a crèche if mums want to do aerobics, zumba, swimming, etc. We have a 25-metre pool plus a small shallow one for babies and toddlers. Four times a week we have something called 'Bounce' which is a soft play area in one of the studios upstairs. In the café there's a small play area so that mums can sit and have a coffee in peace. That's for the tiny ones. We also run a pre-school gym for two to four year olds. We do gymnastics for older children and swimming lessons and there are football training sessions for up to sixteen year olds.

We run a club three times a week for the over-fifties though most of them are seventy as they've come along for years. They do keep fit, badminton, squash or table tennis and congregate afterwards for a cup of coffee in the café, so it's a good physical and social time. They are a lovely bunch of people, we've got to know them and they know us pretty well.

All our classes are open to males and females; we do circuit training – things like body pump, where you use weights – which is very popular with men and there is indoor football and cricket, basketball. So we've a lot going on and evenings tend to be busier than daytime. Outside are tennis and netball courts, football pitches, I don't think there is anything we haven't got.

My badge says 'Customer Advisor, Reception'. I'm supervisor now so do the recruiting and training of new staff and for gym reception upstairs. I also work out the shifts, getting people to cover all of them. The rota lets everyone know their shifts for the following week but we do have extra hours. The first shift starts at 7 a.m., the last finishes at 10.30 p.m. and we're open 7 days a week. It can be quite a difficult, frustrating task at times. We do have a lot of staff, plus contracted and casual staff who get called in two or three times a month, maybe more.

We practise fire drills every Friday morning but warn everyone over the loudspeakers that it is a test alarm. Maintenance men check everything. Sometimes there have been false alarms and we've had to evacuate the building and all staff help out; carrying babies from the crèche is our first port of call, as well as helping the less able. Luckily it's never happened for real and we're pleased with the smooth way our emergency drills work. The fire brigade still turns up for the false alarms – they don't mind.

No two days are the same here, because you meet different people every day with the wide range of activities happening and at the weekend it is different again. That gets extremely busy so swimmers wear coloured bands for timed sessions.

Obviously things don't always run smoothly. Customers can get annoyed and make complaints which are what we receptionists have to deal with, being the first point of contact. But I love my job, it's a great place to work.

PAT NASH
née Huntley

My friend Janet Evans kept saying I should go in for the Junior Carnival Princess Competition. I didn't want to because I was quite shy in those days. I was ten, coming up to eleven that summer in 1962.

However, it was lovely being a carnival princess, the adults on our float took good care of me. Margaret Hazel, whose father owned Hazel the chemists, was carnival queen and the senior princess was Margaret Collins. In those days they had a carnival prince and that year it was Geoffrey Haskell. I'd never had such a pretty dress before. We girls were all in silver lamé and I think the queen had a cape made of purple velvet; I had a stole of purple velvet with the gorgeous silver lamé on the inside and a crown with the same velvet threaded through.

Carnival queen and princesses, 1947.
(Hampshire Museums and Archives)

Galleon carnival float, 1970s. (Hampshire Museums and Archives)

Bands played and there were always spectacular floats from the railway, Pirelli, Warner Lamberts (where I went on to work years later), etc. It was a wonderful experience, apart from being hit by the coins!

We went to tour different places with the carnival. I remember visiting the railway where my Dad worked so he was thrilled, and Moorgreen Hospital at West End. We went into Caustons and they printed my name out on a metal plate. Once those big organisations closed, Eastleigh Carnival was never quite the same. In fact, my son said yesterday that this year's procession has been cancelled due to health and safety. I'm not sure whether he's kidding me or not.

I was still in Cranbury Road School in 1962, having a birthday at the end of August meant I was always the youngest in my class. I remember Miss Brown. She was probably only in her fifties or sixties but looked as if she was 100. She permanently had her hair in a bun, wore a large coat and dragged a shopping trolley behind her. She was pretty scary! She certainly taught me my times tables through fear. We almost sang them out as she walked around the desks and I'd be thinking of the numbers in advance because I daren't get it wrong. But there were some lovely teachers there. In the infants was Mrs Hicks, whose family owned a sweet shop in Chandler's Ford and at Christmas time she'd bring in a suitcase full of sweets and you could go up and choose a couple of things. Miss Bissett was my first teacher and she smacked me quite often. I was a child who got caught when naughty children didn't.

There was a radiator in a room near the boiler and those little bottles of milk were kept there. They were always warm and tasted horrible. But it was a great school, I felt rather sad when the juniors' site became flats.

I went to Chamberlayne Road School for Girls when I moved up to secondary but the following year we were the original pupils to amalgamate at the new Alderman Quilley School. This was my first experience of mixed education – at home I only had sisters so boys were another species to me. The teacher thought it very funny sitting me next to a boy called Ian Palmer; she loved to say 'You two! Huntley and Palmer!' This boy broke my pencils in half whenever he got the opportunity. But I obviously got used to boys as I married fairly young in 1970.

CHRIS SMITH

We always lived in Bishopstoke where I went to the infant school, then Stoke Park Junior School , passing my 11+ in 1966. I cycled to Barton Peveril Grammar School, as it used to be, for six years. My final year was the last new intake of grammar school pupils, it became a college after that.

As a young man, I worked in different towns but wanted to return. I've worked for the Borough Council for twenty-six years now and live in the centre of Eastleigh.

One distinct early memory is that of the old library by the town hall because the door latch seemed ever so high and made a loud noise when you pushed it down. I also recall the distinctive smell of the library.

I spent many happy hours at the Bishopstoke swimming pool. The shop sold mugs of Bovril and packets of crisps. Cubicles with blue wooden swing-doors went all the way round the outside. The older kids sunbathed on top of the cubicles and there was a grass area for people to lie on.

What I remember most is cycling back home from there one glorious Saturday afternoon to watch a World Cup football match on TV on 23 July 1966, which England won 1–0.

As a child I didn't spend much time in Eastleigh itself. I played in the woods at Bishopstoke and there was a field at the bottom of our road where we played football, etc. We'd be there from nine in the morning until it got dark and our parents didn't worry. Occasionally we'd all club together and hire a pitch at Fleming Park, we thought that was brilliant. I only remember good weather as a kid.

I can recall when they closed the Bishopstoke railway bridge for quite a time; you can imagine the chaos that caused, being the main route in from that direction. I'd have to cycle over the wooden slats.

An unusual sight at Bishopstoke swimming pool, an employee's child has a swim before opening time. (George Brooks)

My mother, Vera, still lives in Bishopstoke and in the garage are height measurements that my Dad would take, all written on the wall in his beautiful copperplate writing; e.g 'Chris, 1966, 4' 10"' and now of course the grandchildren. Dad died four years ago, so that handwriting is a wonderful memento.

I think Eastleigh has made great strides. The Swan Centre is over twenty years old and still looks in good condition. It's been a difficult thing to do but Eastleigh has slowly changed its image.

JULIA ALLAN

talks about the work of 'One Community'

Icome from Suffolk but had family in Winchester. In 1980, a job opportunity came along in Winchester so we headed for Hampshire. We chose a house in Eastleigh because it was affordable and seemed a good place to bring up a family – the hunch proved to be correct. When my children (the youngest is now seventeen and the eldest twenty-three) were growing up, there were young families around and a good choice of toddler groups and playgroups, plus excellent schools. The children made many friends and always had plenty to do. So, yes, I think Eastleigh is a great place to live and ideal for travelling. You've two motorways, the trains, the airport; it's quite a hub.

One Community (formerly Eastleigh Community Services) was started in 1978 by Peter Molyneux of Chandler's Ford and it's gone from strength to strength. We have well over 200 member groups now. The organisation's had a couple of name-changes since I began working part-time sixteen years ago. As the children grew older I gradually increased my hours and am now a full-time Operations Manager in Volunteering & Information, so I've grown into One Community, which I'm very passionate about.

One Community has many projects including the Carers' Centre, Young Carers, Care & Respite, Lifeline, the Volunteer Centre, our fleet of community minibuses, Dial-A-Ride and Shopmobility. The list goes on. We also run day centres for older, frail people, including days for people with dementia.

We provide support services to community groups, and information and support for individuals, including information on benefits and help with form-filling. A vibrant community is our aim and we work across the whole Borough of Eastleigh, so if we see a gap in services then we do our best to set something up.

No. 16 Romsey Road,
home of 'One Community'.

The newest service we provide is Macmillan Solutions. It's a pilot in partnership with Macmillan Cancer Support to help people who've been diagnosed with cancer and their friends and relatives. This is split into three types of help: emotional – putting them in touch with somebody they can talk to, to share their feelings and fears; practical help – when somebody is ill and receiving treatment they might find it difficult to mow the lawn, walk the dog, keep on top of the housework so we have volunteers who'll do this for them; and thirdly financial assistance can be available. For instance, we had a lady who, due to her condition, needed to use her washing machine constantly. Then it broke down, but we were able to provide and install a replacement. It's so satisfying to help someone in that sort of predicament. We've trained over twenty volunteers for the scheme and a Macmillan Solutions project is also being piloted in Manchester. Hopefully the scheme can then be rolled out all over the country and it's very exciting to be taking part.

I am a volunteer myself, for Eastleigh Good Neighbours. There are Good Neighbour groups all across Eastleigh Borough and they are trying to set up a group in West End at the moment. Some people don't have family or friends locally, can't get out and are on their own. Not just older people either, sometimes mothers and children. The work is mostly driving, taking people who can't manage public transport to medical centres, hospitals, or shopping. Our volunteer will pick the person up, take them to their appointment and wait for them. This gives a feeling of being supported, especially if their doctor has just told them bad news. The person doesn't feel so alone. In Eastleigh we ask passengers to make a donation. Some pay a little, some pay more and it all works out to cover the costs. Good Neighbours also offer a shopping service for the housebound.

Some of our Good Neighbour volunteers do light gardening. Being unable to manage their garden is a big problem for some older people. Seeing the garden looking good again really cheers them up and also helps them remain independent at home. Gardening help is a service we are trying to extend.

At One Community we have volunteers who fit Lifelines which is very important. Lifelines are pendants or bracelets for vulnerable people. If they have a fall or feel very unwell, they don't have to get to their phone, just press the button on their lifeline.

Before moving to Romsey Road in 1996, One Community (then called Eastleigh Community Services) was divided between two buildings, part was in the old town hall in Leigh Road and the other on the opposite side of the road. Here at no. 16 we feel privileged to work in such beautiful surroundings. It was built in the Edwardian era as a family home, obviously an affluent family who could afford park views from the front balconies and veranda. The house had been empty for a while, the last owners being solicitors, Maund McLeonards.

We were extremely lucky back in the 1990s to receive a lottery grant which means we own it and don't pay rent. It's an asset that also provides office accommodation for tenants and various small organisations have been based here.

The central banister is so warm and inviting and people love to feel the polished wood. There is a wonderful room downstairs, which I imagine was a dining room. It is now a large meeting room called the Molyneux room. Our meeting rooms are available to member groups for their committees or AGMs.

It's always a pleasure to come to work and although these are difficult times there are many good things ahead.

KAY PARTRIDGE
née Francis

I grew up at no. 76 Leigh Road, opposite the Pirelli wall. We were always aware of the traffic so were never allowed bikes out. What I remember is the road floods. As kids we watched out of the window, cars were driving through deep water then breaking down. People walked through the gardens because pavements were covered as well. It happened once on Romsey Road, which was our homeward route from the original Crescent School and we were wading knee-deep. I think the drainage has improved now.

On the water theme, when we were little we loved going to the paddling pool at Fleming Park. It was circular and always had green slime on the bottom. It's been poshed up a lot now, always clean and well-kept. We also paddled in the stream and enjoyed jumping across at the narrow parts.

My teenage years in Eastleigh seemed quite dull. I remember queueing all the way down Market Street to see *Star Wars* and *Grease* at the Regal. Some girls at school petitioned for it to remain a cinema but it became Martine's nightclub. After I left Toynbee Secondary School in 1982 I worked as a nanny in Romsey.

My mother went to live in Scarborough and others in the family followed. I missed them so when the little girl I looked after started school, off I went, aged twenty-one, to Yorkshire. I gained three children and a northern accent in those seventeen years I was there, but always felt a draw to come back to Eastleigh. So did my sister. The time never seemed right until my middle child was due to change to senior school.

Not a lot seem to have changed, Mr Fleat was still headmaster at the Crescent School. What a great teacher he was with an excellent sense of humour but he stood no nonsense. He was unforgettable and he and Mrs Fleat retired in 2010.

The Pirelli wall at Leigh Road. (Len Harvell)

Before we left, the Swan Centre was underway. It was complete on our return in 2005. Lots of new houses and flats had appeared, of course, and even more since we moved back.

We'd always attended church events, I returned to All Saints' Church and after a couple of weeks it was as if I'd never been away. People knew who I was even though I hadn't been around all those years.

I now look after my two teenagers and an eight-year-old on my own, working part-time as a personal assistant. I help a disabled lady whose three-year-old needs a constant eye kept on her. I've always worked with children and find it very satisfying.

We've been in Grantham Road for three years, Desborough Road before that. Mum's back down too, and lives just around the corner. I remember other children asking me when I was little, 'Aren't you scared of your mother?' She was a teacher and they were obviously wary, but to me, she was just my Mum. I'm happy and settled in Eastleigh, my instinct to return was definitely the right thing to do.

JASON EVANS

My father worked at Pirelli in Aberdare, South Wales, but that closed down in 1984. Quite a few people transferred to Eastleigh and Dad was one of them. I was seven at the time and our first home here was in Desborough Road where I went to Norwood Primary School.

Initially I didn't like Eastleigh because I was used to mountains and countryside, living in a small community village where it was safe enough for kids to go out and play. Down here seemed very built-up and claustrophobic though, as my parents consoled, you don't have to walk far to be out in the countryside. Just go over the railway bridge and you're by the River Itchen. We did many river walks as a family.

My homesickness disappeared with the discovery of the airport. I'd never seen planes up close where we'd lived in the Welsh Valleys and was amazed by them. How could they stay up in the air like that? My friend Mark and I started spending a lot of time at the airport which back then was much smaller and friendlier. I think its character has been lost now where it's got so large. There was a big viewing area upstairs where you could sit and watch the planes and nobody bothered you. If they see you hanging around now you get security people pouncing on you. When we were kids we even got invited into the cockpits, either by waiting around to ask a pilot or going to the check-in desk. In those days there were many different airlines, Air UK was the main one and so many different types of planes would fly in. The F27 was the mainstay – the full name is Dutch but sounds like a rude word in English (Fokker). As you can imagine, we kids found that hilarious. Yes, so many types of planes: Heralds, Viscounts, Hawker Siddeley 748s were just a few and even a Douglas VC3 Dakota was there, an old plane used in the Second World War then used for pleasure flights. These days it's nearly all Flybe. I literally lived at the airport as a young boy. We knew members of staff by first name and they knew us. It goes to show how things have

Southampton (Eastleigh) Airport: an aerial view from 1966. (BAA Southampton)

changed, because my Mum would ring the reception desk and they'd put an announcement over the tannoy system 'Ding dong. Would Jason Evans go home please? It's dinner-time.' Can you imagine that happening now?

The air crew did use us a bit as child labour. We'd collect up any old in-flight mags from the cabins and replace them with new ones, that sort of thing, and they'd give us a packet of peanuts and the privilege of sitting in the cockpit. We did it because we loved being around the planes. It seems strange now I'm thirty-four, remembering new planes arriving at the airport that you don't see nowadays, because they're obsolete, too old.

Once we were wandering around and spotted a hangar door left open so strolled in. The men inside never told us off but said, 'Hullo boys, what would you like to have a look at?' Nowadays you'd be escorted off by armed guards. So yeah; Eastleigh was a plane and trainspotters paradise. I enjoyed trainspotting too.

One of my first memories of Eastleigh is the day the parish church caught fire in 1985. It was a sunny day, we were in the back garden and noticed a big black plume of smoke, then heard all the sirens. We walked over to the park to watch the drama of it all, like so many people did.

One of my hobbies is astronomy although Eastleigh is not the best place for this because of the light pollution which you get in any town. They have made improvements, especially in the estate where I live. Our street lights are eco-friendly. I get a few funny looks now and again when I wander through the town carrying my telescope, as if I'm a spy! But my telescope is pointed upwards, into the sky, not at people or places.

Some time ago, they wanted to build on the land of the old allotments and local people created a lot of fuss, petitions to Downing Street, etc. However,

Parish church fire damage, 21 July 1985. (Len Harvell)

they lost the battle. Allotments were then created near the Lakeside Railway; we were lucky to get one and there's a long waiting list now for them. At one time it was beautifully peaceful there, with a big field of sweetcorn nearby. That's been developed on, which is a shame. I grow potatoes, onions, garlic and asparagus and at the moment I'm overloaded with parsnips so offer them to anyone – shame to waste them.

I belong to the Eastleigh District Disability Forum where we work towards making life better for disabled people in Eastleigh. I'm also on the Eastleigh Access Planning Group. If somebody submits plans for a public building, for instance, then a group of us with different disabilities will use their expertise and experience on wheelchair access and signage, e.g. is it easy to read and suitably placed? That's good because you feel you can make a difference. Once I was at the train station and noticed that the high-visibility yellow lines for visually impaired people and general safety were getting faint so I mentioned it to the person in charge. Within a month brand new yellow stripes were painted.

I have a learning disability, something like Asperger's. If a subject interests me, I can learn all about it and become quite knowledgeable. I'm very good with facts, not with figures and common sense isn't so brilliant! This makes it difficult to find a job so I concentrate on keeping busy.

I'm not a night owl these days. I'm not that sociable and don't like places where fights might break out because people can't handle their drink. The new leisure facilities at the Swan Centre were badly needed. Now we have a multiplex cinema, bowling alley and new restaurants which makes a lot of difference when you have friends come to stay because you have somewhere local to take them. Before we'd have to travel into Southampton or Winchester. I'd say today's Eastleigh is a good town, has a lot going for it.

I've lived in a lot of places here, especially during a rebellious phase in my teens. But for the last seven years I have been on the Park 21 Estate which is built on the old Pirelli site. The road names are linked to cabling, like Drum, Bright Wire, Stranding. I'm very happy in my top-floor flat – handy for my telescope! The road leading into the estate is called Pluto Road, not after a planet or cartoon character but 'Pipe Line Under The Ocean'.

CHRIS FRIEND

I've been coming here to Eastleigh Lakeside Railway since I first learned to walk, as long as I can remember. I was born in 1990, and have lived in Chandler's Ford all my life. As soon as I was able, at the age of sixteen, I've worked as a volunteer. I just love it and do as much as I can but obviously don't get any payment for it. I've been a student in London, so help out when I'm at home. I drive the miniature steam trains and I guard, clip the tickets and wave the flag. I'm in charge of organising the volunteers and also run the Footplate Experience Course. People pay to come along for a day and learn how to drive the steam engines. That's good fun.

I try to do one whole day a week, help out in the workshop and obviously at the weekend, as we're only open to the public then, except during school holidays. I never work out how long I spend here, in case I get a shock, but would say between 8 and 16 hours a week. My ambition is to drive full-size trains and am now applying for jobs, trying to break my way in.

Why do I love it so much? It's difficult to define but a steam engine is like a living being. You have to wake it up, put the fire in it, get it going. There's a great skill in driving it, the engine and driver have to be as one to get the best out of each other.

I love the people here. That's a huge attraction; everyone is so friendly and enthusiastic. There's between thirty and forty volunteers, some come and go. Then we have three paid engineers in the workshop during the week. It's a non-profit organisation and any money gets ploughed back in; we can't afford to pay too many people, just enough the keep the railway running safely. We all do it for love. We come here and have fun while getting on with the work. We have a few female volunteers, one who drives and helps out in the workshop. Others help in the shop.

The grounds are operated by the Country Parks; we just look after the track and any grass growing close to that, keeping it neat and tidy. We have

Chris Friend, engine driver at Lakeside Railway. (Chris Friend)

volunteers who do the flowers outside; there is always a colourful display which looks welcoming.

It's brilliant when we host school trips, the children are so thrilled. I love to see people enjoying what we have here. I get so much from it myself, it's good to see other people feel the same. It's great when we're really busy, there's always a wonderful atmosphere. We did really well the last Easter when we had a record-breaking amount of sunshine for April, but I love it whatever the weather.

THE COLIN FIRTH
CONNECTION

Eastleigh made the headlines in 2011 when actor Colin Firth won an Oscar, a Bafta and Golden Globe for his role in *The King's Speech*. In the Hollywood Walk of Fame a star was laid proclaiming his name and he's also been given the Freedom of the City of London. He was born and spent most of his childhood in Grayshott, near Winchester.

We all remember how Colin became a mega heart-throb in 1995 when he appeared as Mr Darcy in the BBC's serialisation of *Pride and Prejudice*. Apparently he had the same affect on female pupils at Barton Peveril Sixth Form College where he studied A Level English Literature, Religious Studies and Drama from 1977 to 1979. His talent for the stage shone through in college productions of *Scapino* by Molière and *Sweeney Todd*.

Jonathan Prest, the headmaster, nominated Colin for the famous alumni award from the Association of Colleges in 2010. He said, 'Our former pupil is a very agreeable and pleasant person. He's a good conversationalist and interested in all sorts of topics, not just acting but the rights of refugees and Fair Trade. He's been a great inspiration to our drama students.' So in June that year Colin was reunited with his former English teacher when he received the Gold Award from the Association. In his acceptance speech at the House of Commons, Colin acknowledged the important role she played in his career and how the support from all his teachers motivates him still, more than thirty years later.

'I have to say that my time at Barton Peveril is probably among the two happiest years of my life. I probably owe the most to an extremely fine English teacher, Penny Edwards. I must have paid attention because I can still quote randomly from Thomas Hardy and Byron, which gives the impression I've read a great deal more than I have!'

Left: *Colin Firth as a teenage student in the late 1970s. (Barton Peveril College)*

Right: *Colin Firth reunites with his English teacher, Penny Edwards. (Barton Peveril College)*

Penny, whose career at Barton Peveril spanned thirty-six years, said of Colin, 'He was a very sociable student and a lot of the girls liked him. He was very sensitive to literature and certainly had stage presence. Underneath the long-haired, laddish exterior was quite a shrewd character who knew exactly what he wanted to do. His well-deserved success comes as no surprise. It's quite something to sit in a packed cinema on a weekday afternoon and watch your former pupil give what so many critics clearly believe to be the performance of a lifetime.'

Sue Overell, of West End, who was one year below him at college, appeared on local television with a diary from her Barton Peveril school days. She'd written, 'Saw Colin Firth in the school production of *Sweeney Todd* and he was amazing.' Sue told how he was very popular, 'Not just with the girls, there was always a crowd around him in the common room. We all thought he would go on to be a star.'

Author's note: I have not even attempted to contact the busy actor himself for this book, but shook the hand of a young man who shook the hand . . .

MIKE PARKER

I came to Barton Peveril College in 2008, having been in Wildern School, Hedge End, where I was born and brought up. I chose this college because of its high reputation for drama and studied A Level Drama Theatre Studies and B. Tech Performing Arts. They have a wonderful theatre, studios, gifted teachers and alumni. That time has been the greatest two years of my life so far. The course revitalised me, especially in the career sense. When I started here I wasn't sure where I wanted my future to go. The teachers gave me confidence in myself.

I've just taken a gap year to concentrate on applying to drama schools and am thrilled to have a place at East 15, in north-east London, which is one of the top UK drama schools. This will be a three-year course and hopefully after graduating I will fulfil my dreams of being a professional actor.

I've done loads of acting here in Barton Peveril, my favourite and strongest performance being in *The Laramie Project*. I've also been in six different productions down in Portsmouth during my gap year.

How did I meet and shake the hand of Colin Firth? It was connected to his award from the Association of Colleges. Colleges in the UK can nominate a former pupil who has gone on to excel in their field. The AOC organise a 'Mini Me' scheme which means the nominating college pick a current student they believe has similar aspirations and think will go far, akin to the person who's won the award. It was a great honour to be chosen as the 'Mini Me' and a good confidence boost as well. I went to the House of Commons with Mr Prest, the headmaster, Carol Geddes, the Communications Director, plus some others for the ceremony. There were about five awards but Colin Firth was the most high-profile. The idea of the 'Mini Me' programme is that you meet the person you'd like to live up to. So I met Colin who gave me lots of good advice, acting tips, particularly about the future and how to get into the business. He was really nice, an absolute inspiration. Then back in February among all the

Mike Parker meets Colin Firth at the House of Commons, 2010. (Mike Parker)

Oscar hype I was asked to appear on *Daybreak*, ITV, which was good experience. I was so thrilled he won an Oscar; he deserved it for that amazing performance in *The King's Speech*. I'd been taken aback when I met him because he's such a humble guy, very down to earth, despite being a Hollywood celebrity he behaved just normal, like any other man in the street.

Strangely enough, a couple of weeks ago I went to East 15 Acting School to watch a showcase and look at where I'll be training next year. My Dad nudged me – Colin Firth was sitting in the row behind us. During the interval, I walked down the corridor and he was leaning against a wall. He looked at me, put his hand up as if to say 'Don't I know you from somewhere?' I said, 'Hullo. We met a year ago. I was your "Mini Me".'

'Ah, yes,' he said, then we had a good old chat. I didn't even expect him to recognise me but he was very friendly. We talked about Barton Peveril again, which he obviously regards very highly. I told him about my gap year and how I'd be attending East 15 next year and it turns out his son is going there too.

So I'll obviously bump into him again. It's a small world and a privilege to have this link with him.

Where do I see myself? I don't really have a main goal, though I'd love to do well in theatre. As they say, theatre's the buzz, screen is the money. I've done a bit of paid screen acting this year, short documentaries and the like. My main dream is to perform in the National Theatre. I've gone there many times and the thought of treading those boards like so many excellent actors from the past, well that's something else.

But back to reality, what Colin Firth said to me was, 'The acting journey is a long slog. Everyone starts off on an equal playing field and you have to work your way to the top in an extremely competitive profession. You have to be incredibly patient. You might just appear in three adverts a year. You persistently work your way to get merited in places and recognised. Stick to what you know, stick to what you believe in and keep your feet right on the ground.'

CASSIDY

aged almost eight

It's my birthday in two weeks' time and yesterday we went to the Pound Shop to buy things for the party bags. I remember when it was Woolworths. I'm having a dance mat party at Fleming Park where everyone stands on their own mat which has squares on and a big screen tells you where to jump. It's really fun.

I like dancing, and had lessons at Leigh Road Ballroom, won some rosettes and a trophy. We were all very upset when that had to close down. It's a youth club now.

When the cinema opened in the Swan Centre, Mum took me to see my first film. It was *Monsters vs Aliens*. Mum and Dad have lived in Dutton Lane for eighteen years, so I've lived in this house all my life. I think our road is pretty. You can walk along the pavement and see the flowers people grow in their front gardens.

I go to the Crescent School in Toynbee Road and next month I'll be in Year 4. I remember my very first day. I woke up early which meant I had to wait ages before getting-up time, then we had omelettes. Next door is my friend Thomas who's the same age, so we started school and sat together. That was nice because you weren't alone. After Years 1 and 2, during the summer holidays, I missed school and wished I could camp there. I like learning. I enjoy doing maths and also playtime is fun with all your friends. Sometimes in class we giggle, because our teacher often double spells on the wipe-board, like 'do do your best', which is wrong and also we're already doing our best! We have assembly every Monday and Wednesday, they're really good, and at the last one, I had to stand up to say a big thank you from everyone as I'm the school councillor in my class.

A Spitfire flies over Dutton Lane, drawn by Cassidy.

We have lots of lovely times. There's always 'The Crescent's Got Talent Competition'. A five-year-old won this year, she stood up in front of the whole school and sang!

I also got through in the Sophie Barringer Trust Dance Competition. She was a girl at Norwood School who died of cancer. That makes you feel very sad.

This summer I'm enjoying the holidays. I like whizzing along on my scooter and taking our puppy Rocco for a walk by the river with Dad and my brother. There's also the Library Challenge. You go to the library in the Swan Centre and choose six books. When you take one back, you tell the lady all about it and she gives you a badge. When you've read all six you get a Circus Stars Certificate.

Soon I'll be taking part in the summer carnival. We're doing a Dr Seuss float. He's a cat who teaches you rhymes and opposites and has lots of friends. I was in the winter carnival and really enjoyed that. Going to the park is nice. The bandstand has been painted yellow, red and green, it used to be black and grey.

Next week I'm having my first sleep-over, just my best friend Macy. That'll be cool. Not sure what I want to do when I grow up. Last year I wanted to be a doctor but I've seen on TV what they have to do. It's disgusting. So perhaps I'll work in a dress shop . . .

ACKNOWLEDGEMENTS

Many thanks to all the people interviewed for this book. It was a pleasure to share their memories and experiences and also to be loaned their personal photographs. It's been a privilege to be invited into their homes, hear their unique stories and be offered lots of cuppas (and biscuits).

Special thanks to the Mallender family for their enthusiasm and encouragement. Also my appreciation goes to: Carol Geddes, Debbie Bourne, Debbie Rigney, David St John, Eastleigh Museum, George Brooks, Jane Flood, Joanne Calcutt, Linda and Len Harvell, Maureen Chapman, Mike Denning, Natalia Benjamin, Sally Johnson, Wendy Bowen, Solent Sky (Alan Mansell), Southampton Writing Buddies and Penny Legg.

Useful websites
www.ageuk.org.uk
www.barton-peveril.ac.uk
www.basquechildren.org/
www.davidstjohn.co.uk/heinz.html
www.eastleigh.gov.uk
www.ihampshire.co.uk/profile/.../Fleming-Park-Leisure-Centre
www.steamtrain.co.uk
www.1community.org.uk
www.spitfireonline.co.uk
www.southamptonairport.com
www.glenjayson.blogspot.com